# WAR:
# A CALL TO THE INNER LAND

# WAR:
# A CALL TO THE INNER LAND

*by*

*Eberhard Arnold*

Preface by John Farina
Introduction by Gordon Zahn

PAULIST PRESS
New York/Mahwah

248.4
Ar W

Library of Congress Cataloging-in-Publication Data
Arnold, Eberhard, 1883–1935.
    War: a call to the inner land.

    Translation of: introd. and chapters 1–3 of Innenland;
with new preface.
    1. Spiritual life. I. Title.
BV4503.A772513   1986      248.4      86-25216
ISBN 0-8091-2851-9

Published by Paulist Press
997 Macarthur Boulevard
Mahwah, N.J. 97430

Printed and bound in the United States of America

# CONTENTS

Dedicated to my faithful wife
who is the best help on this way.

# PREFACE
## TWENTIETH CENTURY APOCALYPTIC*

*T*HE OBJECT *of the book . . . is to make an appeal
in all the political, social, and economic upheaval
today. It is an appeal for decision in the area of faith
and beliefs, directed to the hearts of all those who do not
want to forget or lose God and His ultimate Kingdom.*

With these words we are ushered into the world
of Eberhard Arnold as disclosed in the most comprehensive and seminal of his many works. The
style of these opening lines is that of a man with
a message; it is direct, abrupt, and almost strident
in tone. It is twentieth century apocalyptic written
as was the writing of a Daniel or an Isaiah to challenge its hearers with a message of impending
judgment and the absolute necessity of radical re-
pentance. But also like the apocalyptic literature
of old, it is, in the final analysis a message of
hope—hope in God's power as the ultimate Lord

*An earlier version of this piece appeared in *The Plough*
(February/March 1986):18–21.

of history, hope in His goodness, and above all hope in His final *hesed,* His loving kindness for His people.

To understand this work, one must understand the context out of which it came. The first edition of *Der Krieg ein Aufruf zur Innerlichkeit* appeared in 1914 as Germany rushed into the First World War as an ally of Austria. The horror of seeing all of Europe engulfed in a conflict of unprecedented size and savagery shocked Arnold. As armies of nearly 4,000,000 men clashed in a futile struggle, the young lecturer turned his attention to the cause of violence in the human heart and its cure. Over the next two decades he refined his thought and this led to the final edition on which this volume is based in 1936.

During the 1930's, moved by a seeming desire for self-destruction, Europe once again moved inexorably toward war. Strained by widespread economic disasters, crazed by promises of power, filled with greed and nationalistic fervor, Europeans during that decade endured the uneasy peace established by "the war to end all wars," and watched as a new breed of dictator arose: Lenin and Stalin in Russia, Franco in Spain, Mussolini in Italy, and in Germany the man who was able to take the strengths of the German people—their love of the Fatherland, their disciplined strength, their romantic aspirations, and their technical inventiveness—and enslave them to his own demonic lust for power: Adolf Hilter. Between 1919 and 1932 Hitler skillfully built up the political base of his Nazi party, winning a majority of votes in the popular elections held that latter year. In 1933 he was named Chancellor, and later that year, after a fire destroyed the Reichstag, he suppressed all opposition and emerged as Führer. Through a skillful campaign he built support, utilizing methods from the Youth Movement and, most effectively, the mass rally. William L. Shirer, the American journalist who later wrote *The Rise and Fall of the Third Reich*, attended a September 1934 Nazi rally in Nuremberg, along with nearly a half-million Germans. He had come to Nuremberg to see first-hand what it was about Hitler that made him so popular. In describing the five-day rally he turned repeatedly to religious language to express what he was seeing. He told of being caught one night in a mob of 10,000 hysterics jammed into the moat outside Hitler's hotel. When the Führer appeared, the crowd went into a frenzy:

*I was a little shocked at the faces, especially those of the women. . . . They looked up at him as if he were a Messiah, their faces transformed into something positively inhuman.*

The pageantry used by the rally planners conjured up for Shirer suggestions of "the mysticism and religious fervor of an Easter or Christmas

Mass in a great Cathedral." Hitler preached a message that called for surrender of individual concerns for the good of the nation. He spoke of community and providential mission of a coming millennium, of a destiny for Germany. "Under the mystic lights and at the sound of the magic words of the Austrian they were merged completely in the Germanic herd," shedding their individual lives for a new corporate identity free from personal responsibilities and ready to follow their leader with pietistical devotion. To this spectacle of mass persecution, militarism, rabid nationalism, and hate-mongering the established Christian churches responded, by and large, with silence at best and outright complicity at worst.

Eberhard Arnold uttered an absolute no to all this. He chose a prophetic alternative to the madness he saw all around him, a madness that the established churches seemed happy to accept. He found himself comfortable only with the radical Anabaptist approach to the Church-State question, and thereby rejected the Nazi claims that they were God's special agents doing His providential bidding. His strenuous refusal of all attempts by the government to use religion for its own ends was a witness of unmistakable clarity and strength.

Throughout *Inner Land* Arnold is constantly countering and correcting the Nazis' efforts to capture the souls of Germans. The future, which Hitler was painting as a time of new greatness for Germany, Arnold referred to as a time of "God's approaching judgment." Here his apocalyptic style is most evident. He warns of impending suffering and doom; no good can come of the insane militarism, of the expansionism and avarice, only sure destruction. Whereas Hilter was hailed as a new king of a glorious German empire, Arnold spoke uncompromisingly of the "ultimate Kingdom" which was only God's. History pointed not to the rise of Germany but to God's Kingdom as the great Omega point. The German people's mission was not to rule the earth as a new superrace but "to lead to the inner land of the invisible, to God and the Spirit . . . to show a way to new love." Instead of yielding up their wills to their political leaders, Arnold urged his countrymen to pay heed to their consciences. He devoted two entire chapters to a discussion of the conscience and its role in aiding the individual to clearly discern the difference between the Holy Spirit and the evil spirit—a difference that the Nazis were expert at blurring.

In the face of a national call to join the Nazis in their new German nation, Arnold offered a different picture of community. His community was to be characterized not by a superiority, but by an awareness of the essential unity that binds all people. In place of concupiscence, he offered self-giving charity that expressed itself in voluntary poverty. By giving oneself to this community— this Church of Christ, this Kingdom of God—one emerged, not as a peon of the State, whose will and conscience had been silenced, but as a mature person, restored to the image of the Creator, free to live and free to love.

This book evidences not only the political context out of which it came, but also the rich sources on which Arnold drew. The famous fourteenth-century Dominican mystic, Meister Eckhart, is a favorite inspiration for much of the book's doctrine of detachment. This Rhinelander had a sense of the mystery of the Godhead, of the importance of emptying ourselves of all possessions and attachments to this world before approaching the ineffable God, whose ways appear to us as "darkness." But Arnold grows uncomfortable with Eckhart's stress on the passive dimension of the contemplative life and shows himself once again more the prophet than the mystic. An "active stillness," he writes, "leads believers to work for the world in such a way that they do not become wholly 'worldly,' and yet they never become inactive." In fact many of the great contemplatives of the Middle Ages like Eckhart were anything but inactive, and one senses that it is Arnold's prophetic urgency more than the all-too-common evangelical prejudice against Catholics that led him to neglect this; his writing is filled with irenic apeals for unity and shows an animus for no one except those who would misuse the Gospel to their own ends. He stands rather as a balance, a middle way, between the contemplative and activist traditions. On the one hand he repeatedly insists on the primacy of the inner life. He speaks of "the heart," "the soul," and "the spirit," in addition to "the inner life": all are overlapping terms, each is merely another linguistic tool he uses to dig deeper to the core of the human experience of God. He emphasizes the need for grace, and for the power of God. On the other hand, he rejects a radical passivity, whether based on an appeal to mystical experience as we have seen, or on a Reformed doctrine of total depravity that would minimize the power of the will as a force for good or the importance of good works. Action was a moral imperative for Arnold—and here one sees the impact of Kant on his thought. The ideal of Christianity must take form—tangible, concrete form in the present.

This same incarnational realism that so permeates this work informs Arnold's understanding of revelation. A later edition is subtitled "A Guide to the Heart and Soul of the Bible," a title that by one way of reckoning seems out of place, since the work spends relatively little time talking about the Bible, *per se*. The subtitle is, rather, a hermeneutical statement; it implies that this book is what the Bible—not a certain chapter or verse, but the whole of it—means for today. This is what God's word means for those who would hear it now. This is the word made flesh. Here again Arnold appears as prophet, delivering his "thus saith the Lord" to his countrymen. But it is not as a self-proclaimed Teutonic Messiah, but merely as a witness to the truth that he comes.

It is that witness with all its intensity and ceaseless scrutiny that makes this book extraordinary. That witness was a product of a time when the issues of life and death were writ boldly on the face of history. This book shows us clearly that the forces of horror and inhumanity that wartime manifests are grounded in the heart. But it shows us also that the capacity to respond to God's Spirit and counter those destructive powers that would threaten to engulf us lies there as well.

*John Farina*

*This is the covenant I will make with the House of Israel after those days, says the Lord: I will put my Law within them and write it in their hearts; I will be their God and they shall be my people!*

# INTRODUCTION

It would be difficult to exaggerate the importance of *Inner Land* to Eberhard Arnold and to those who have developed and preserved his vision in the Bruderhof communities. At least that is the conclusion one draws from its history. For one thing, there were three editions—1918, 1923, and 1932—prepared (one assumes with revisions) by the author in addition to its original appearance in 1914 under the title, *War, A Challenge to Inner Awareness.* Though incomplete at the time of Arnold's death, the complete Fourth Edition appeared in 1936 and was republished in an American edition in 1975 in English.

The value placed by his successors upon what may be taken as the definitive statement of Arnold's spiritual heritage may be seen in the care taken to preserve it in its integrity and promote its spread. A touch of drama was added when the nearly complete printing of the fifth edition (counting *War* as the first) faced possible confiscation by the Nazis in 1933. To avoid this, the members of the Bruderhof community, then located in the Rhoen hills of Germany buried the finished portions of the run in metal boxes. The following year they were taken from their hiding place and sent in small packages to their newly established Alm community in Liechtenstein. Already alert to the difficulties they would face under the Third Reich, that second community had been formed as a haven for their children and the young men who would be subject to military service. This was but the beginning of the hardships and wanderings the future was to hold. Although their revered founder would die before their troubles began in earnest, the teachings set forth in *Inner Land* would continue to guide and inspire in the days of struggle and sacrifice they would be called upon to endure.

What we have here is but the first part, or volume, of what is considered a 5-volume work. The whole is subtitled "A Guide into the Heart and Soul of the Bible," but one is cautioned not to expect the systematic exegesis this might imply. Instead Arnold is concerned with setting forth what might better be described as the "spirit" of the New Testament and relating that to his conceptualization of what the behavior of the committed Christian should be.

To some readers his ideas will seem excessive in their piety or too abstract in generalization. Even so, they deserve a careful reading if for no other reason than they provide the key to the continued existence and vitality of the Bruderhof communities and their character as a religious social movement. Though each separate community— there are four in the United States at the present writing—is what the social scientist would describe as an "intentional community" in its own right, the closeness of contact and unity of purpose and belief among them justifies the broadened category. In their ties with the older Hutterite tradition (briefly interrupted but in full effect again) they represent a religious "denomination" as well, of course, but the respect they have earned and the influence they have had upon segments of the broader American national consciousness justifies treating the Bruderhof communities—and Arnold's writings—in a separate context from the older Anabaptist groups with which they are in fraternal union.

A more compelling justification rests with Eberhard Arnold himself and his role as creative founder and, even a half century after his death, inspiring teacher. From his own autobiographical sketches and the accounts of his widow (who died in 1980 at the age of 95) we get a picture of a "God-obsessed" man who was able to reach out and set others afire with his ideas.

Contemporary biographers of psychiatric bent might have a field day with the sixteen-year-old boy stretched out on the floor of his room with his face pressed against the boards trying to free himself of guilt for allowing a statue of Venus to incite desires that threatened to detract from "the pure and innocent love of Jesus." Even before, he had challenged his father, "a scholarly, high-ranking Church official," on what he, Eberhard, felt to be the failure of established religion to concern itself more with social injustice and to return to the pure simplicity of the life and practices of the early Christians.

These themes were to dominate his religious thinking throughout his entire life. As a student he attached himself to groups and individuals committed to similar religious interests and became a leader among his peers who shared his interest in spiritual study and exploration. He met the young woman who was to become his wife at one such conference, and it is clear that it was this convergence of interest in things religious that brought them together—and kept them together. The published volume of their engagement letters reveals two young people exchanging spiritual reflections and scriptural interpretations instead of the usual sentimentalities and romantic flourishes one would ordinarily expect to find in such communications.

All of which has much to do with the volume at hand and, of course, the complete work of which it is a part. It is the mature expression—Arnold was in his thirty-first year when the first version was published—of the concerns and yearnings that had already dominated his early teens. Whatever changes one might trace in the subsequent editions were in the nature of expanded interpretations and applications to the changes that had taken place in society. They undoubtedly reflect the new insights and experiences gained from the life and trials in the early Bruderhof communities, but there is little question that the overall thrust and message remained unchanged.

The title is the key, and this is particularly true if one refers to the German title: *Innenland.* Translation does not do the term full justice. The "inner land" or "land within" concepts come close enough if one takes them with reference to the person identifying them with himself or herself alone. The social scientist would perhaps prefer to speak of "inner space," conceptualizing that as the aspect of every individual which must always lie beyond the reach of the outsider, a space to be preserved and protected against the threat of intrusion from without or, even worse, the loss or betrayal of one's personal integrity. To the social psychologist this inviolable "inner realm" is the core of the personality; to Eberhard Arnold it was the residence of the soul.

Allowing for the difference in contexts the two are the same. In the Preface to the 1932 edition Arnold makes the point that he seeks no confrontation with psychology. It is intriguing to speculate on the use he might have made of the new and more subtle concepts and techniques available to today's psychologists in their efforts to probe more deeply into the mysteries of this *"Innenland."* Would his conclusions have been different? Probably not. Would they find a more receptive audience had he made use of them? Possibly yes. As it is there is reason to fear that our more "sophisticated" readers of today (and this includes the religionists among us) might be put off by the style and intensity of his spiritually-oriented terminology. This should not be, of course, and one may hope it will not be the case. Chances are, however, that for far too many it will be, and those who do not make the special effort to let Arnold speak to them in his own way and in his own terms will be the losers.

There is no denying the fact: his is a "hard line" approach. Writing in the shadow of Hitler, he knows the problem. "Our times have once more revealed the state of man's inner life: he is filled with everything but God, who alone fills man's destiny." One must recognize the demands presented by interests other than God's—the individual's own needs and those of the nation and oppressed classes are given explicit recognition— but they are not to be given priority over the demands of God. The only answer to the commotion and confusion surrounding humankind lies in a full conversion. "Rebirth is the only name we can give to such a radical change with its childlike trust in God's intervention and firm, manly expectation of it. This is the complete opposite of the former life. It is only through such a complete change that we—by going through judgment—can recognize in all that happens the approach and intervention of God's rule."

How that complete change is to be accomplished and how expressed is where difficulty can arise. In my own case I must confess to second thoughts and misgivings almost as soon as I agreed to undertake this Introduction. It is not that I expected anything other than what I found, a profound statement of an exceptionally gifted man's theological insights and spiritual commitment. I was familiar enough with Arnold's writings and with their expression in the Bruderhof movement to anticipate a spiritual and intellectual challenge. I was not disappointed.

But the second thoughts and misgivings have not disappeared. They relate not so much to Arnold and his teachings as they do to my own perspective and its possibly fundamental differences from his. We are not at odds about the essentials of what it means to be a Christian in what Thomas Merton has characterized as this "post-Christian era." We are in broad agreement on principles and objectives, especially in our absolute rejection of war and violence. Both of us see the role of the Christian, whether as individual believer or as Church, to be "judge of the nations" and to refuse to cooperate when asked to take part in or support what one knows in his or her heart to be evil. Where our perspectives diverge—and this concerns the nature of Christ's call and the nature of our response to that call—the difference has more to do with range of options and the intensity of obligation. To say that I would consider myself less narrow with respect to the first and more lenient with respect to the second does not diminish my appreciation and admiration for the tighter standards he and his brothers have set.

The sources of the differences in perspective can be identified easily enough. I am, first of all, a Roman Catholic and (unlike a growing number of my co-religionists) still strongly "institutional" in my adherence to that Church, its organizational structure, and its sacramental system. A more difficult chasm to bridge, perhaps, is my personal preference for what is generally referred to (and usually unfavorably today) as "privatized" religious practice in contrast to the "communal" forms of devotion and worship. Finally, and it is possible that Arnold himself would have found this an insurmountable block, as a professional sociologist my approach to expressing the "eternal verities" is more likely to deal with them as ideological and behavioral frameworks for observation and interpretation. Those who think and speak of matters religious in theological/philosophical abstractions often take offense at the social scientist's tendency to put them to the test of observable mundane reality and its behavioral implications. Such "intrusions" into a sphere ordinarily reserved for the mysterious and unmeasurable can be inconvenient.

In one sense, I suspect Arnold would welcome the approach which tests the extent to which professed Christians really practice what they preach. I am not all that sure, however, that he would be equally enthusiastic about applying empirical measures to some of his more inspirational generalizations. Is it true, one might ask, that man's nature cannot be influenced by food taken in by the body or by hygiene or gymnastics? Is it "in distinct opposition to the Word and life of Jesus" to suggest otherwise? I realize, of course, that he is speaking of "human nature" *as such,* but to the social scientist that philosophical concept is suspect and open to empirical challenge.

My purpose here, though, is not to debate but, rather, to define the important areas of convergence that exist despite the admitted differences in perspective. The denominational identification, for example, presents far less of an obstacle in this respect today than might have been true at the time Arnold was writing and revising this most crucial work. Ecumenism, something which at that time was promoted only by people like Max Josef Metzger and others in the "Third Hour" movement, is no longer the far-out radicalism it was considered then. More to the point, however, changes in Roman Catholic teachings and emphasis, attributable in great part to Pope John XXIII and the Council he called, have legitimated options compatible with Arnold's pacifism and total commitment to non-violence—options which, I can testify from my own experience, were simply not recognized as permissible prior to *Pacem in Terris*.

The "institutional" character of Roman Catholicism, especially its patterns of authoritarian discipline, still constitutes a stumbling block to believers in the Anabaptist tradition. We can be confident that Emmy and Eberhard would still maintain "that the 'World Church' stands on a completely wrong foundation because it accepts children into membership in the Christian Church by right of birth instead of their taking this step through their own faith, which alone makes it possible to receive baptism." (Emmy Arnold in *Torches Together*) Since this difference of opinion led to struggles with their own Protestant families, one assumes the "World Church" of which she speaks is not solely or specifically Roman Catholicism, but it clearly applies.

More important, though, another point of disagreement existing between them and their parents (and, without doubt, this would have extended to Roman Catholicism of their day as well) no longer presents as much difficulty today.

Popes, Council, and bishops—not to mention an increasingly vocal and active Catholic laity— would not only be able "to understand our revolutionary approach to the problems of social justice and that of the Church" but would share it, though not in every detail.

As for the mere fact of "institutionalization," that should present no problem at all. It is of the nature of any religious community which achieves some measure of stability and longevity that it tends to become "institutionalized" in its teachings and practice.

It would not be difficult to demonstrate that this is true of the Bruderhof communities— whether it be in manner of dress, distribution of tasks and authority, ceremonial commemorations, and the like. There may be nothing comparable to the fixed ritual and sacramental systems of Roman Catholicism, but I am sure one could discover their counterparts. One might even suggest that, judging from the importance in which they are held, the writings of Eberhard Arnold have become something of a *depositum fidei* for the Movement—and with full justification!

The areas of compatability outweigh the points of difference in scope and, probably, importance as well. Whether it be the "family orientation" of the Bruderhof community or the emphasis placed by Eberhard Arnold on respect for tradition and the legacy of Christianity's past, his writings—and this is especially true of this book—surmount all denominational barriers and can serve as a valuable source of instruction for all who consider themselves followers of Christ.

The second difference in perspective to which I have confessed is probably traceable to my own personality and its early formation. To say I regard religious belief as something preeminently personal and private is not to deny that it gives rise to communal obligations. If I would second the observation of a Franz Jaegerstaetter, the heroic Austrian peasant beheaded for his refusal to serve in Hitler's armed forces, that "as long as we live in this world, I believe it is never too late to save ourselves and perhaps some other soul for Christ," this does not diminish my awareness of a personal responsibility to make that "perhaps" a reality and extend it to as many other souls as possible.

One sometimes encounters interpretations that suggest this is not enough, that only "in community" and by sharing a simple "life-style" does one *really* serve Christ in a true and fitting manner; and this makes me more than a little uncomfortable. This is not to say that Arnold or his successors hold this as a fixed obligation for all, but it is clear (and the Bruderhof communities testify to the fact) that he regarded anything short of this unsatisfactory and incomplete. Which, most will agree, it probably is. Certainly one needs nothing more than a brief visit to one of those communities to sense the depth of Christian commitment and dedication to the service of Christ that is present among its members. At the same time I would insist (and I do not think Arnold would deny) that it is possible, perhaps necessary, for some to "live in the world" and practice their faith in the more private sphere of personal interests and associations. After all, in times of financial stress in the formative days of Bruderhof history, it was often those who did remain "in the world" to whom Eberhard turned for the assistance that made it possible to endure and grow.

But here, too, the differences may be less basic than they appear on the surface. The communal expression of Christian commitment depends, in the last analysis, upon the individual member's relationship in that *Innenland* with his or her God. For the Bruderhof movement to have survived the great tests and tragedies it has faced is evidence of the spiritual strength of those who made the decision to persevere. And there is no doubt that this book, together with Arnold's other writings, provided a strong bond which has served as a source of that strength and the continuity it helped to assure.

Nor is there any doubt that life in community does provide reinforcement for individual commitment. At the same time it should be clear that it is no less true that without such individual commitment a really viable community is not likely to endure for long. This may be taken, I suppose, as a sociological truism. As such it serves to introduce that last, and probably most critical, source of our difference in perspective. But this, too, I would hold, could enhance as well as diminish appreciation of the contribution Eberhard Arnold and his writings have made to the understanding of what the realization of the Christian promise will require.

The "sociological imagination," as C. Wright Mills used the term, seeks to discover the "intersections" between history and biography. To the extent one masters and applies this technique, one is better able to address the major issues of the day (which, to Mills, is the ultimate objective of social science). Eberhard Arnold and his writings, with the Bruderhof communities—or movement—as their incarnation, provide a tempting subject for intensive study and analysis in the Mills formulation.

The temptation must be resisted here for obvious reasons, but some of the things such a study would find significant can be suggested. There is, for instance, the social setting into which Eberhard Arnold was born. This accounted in great part for his early involvement in the intellectual and religious ferment that marked the Germany of that time and, in particular, the academic world in which he was so deeply involved. If it were nothing more than youthful rebellion against perceived parental shortcomings or, as seems to be a more likely explanation, the eager immersion into the flood of new ideas, the attraction of Arnold and his friends (including, of course, the young woman who was to become his fiancée and bride) was perhaps inevitable.

Then, too, there was the disruption of the old order brought about by World War I and its disastrous aftermath. In creating a new life and future, it was only natural that young people who had already found the pre-war society sadly wanting in moral quality would get together and explore other possibilities. The community which was to become the first Bruderhof was the outcome of one such exploration by the Arnolds and close friends. We can be sure that many other, and often quite similar, community ventures of this nature were begun at this time and failed. That theirs did not may be taken as evidence of a deeper source of inspiration. If so, we may be certain that much of that inspiration is to be found in Arnold's leadership and writings.

It worked the other way around as well. The persistence and endurance of the Bruderhof movement despite all the difficulties, external and internal, it has faced enabled it to serve as the vehicle for the perpetuation of Arnold's memory and his writings. Indeed, one must question whether, given the nature of the social setting in which we now exist, he and his works might have much chance of gaining a hearing (much less acceptance) today. Nor is it all that certain that a community founded upon his principles could take root and grow into maturity as the Bruderhof with its five thriving communities in New York, Pennsylvania, Connecticut, and England obviously has done.

A purely physicalist vision of human nature has taken over to a degree Arnold would have found diabolical (as, of course, it may well be). Not only does this orientation dominate the thoughts and actions of "ordinary" people, but it colors those of professional intellectuals, not excluding some of our more prominent *religionists*, as well. Actions once seen as the product of volition and responsible choice are now attributed to the rigid determinism of the laws governing matter. Human beings, once revered as creations but slightly "lower than the angels," are now regarded (and treated!) as nothing more than the highest product (to this point at least) of organic evolution.

The "mystery of sex" is mystery no longer, having been superseded by diagrams in high school biology texts; and in practice it is regarded as little more than a stimulus/response "chemistry" reaction—often enough, indeed, as simply a recreational interlude in casual social encounters. So, too, with the "miracle" of life itself. Once considered as special gift of a loving Creator and, as such, partaking of the sacred, it has become a laboratory exercise, subject to experimentation and manipulation. Given the time and necessary resources, we are assured, there is a real prospect that the life processes themselves can be made completely subject to scientific control. This is sometimes seen as opening the way to the solution of all our problems through the establishment and selection of a "gene pool" that will enable us to fashion a perfect society peopled by individuals produced according to planned number and design. Indeed, modern psychology with its newer techniques of behavior modification has already made it possible to unravel and restructure that "inner land" of the human psyche "on order."

It is not so much the expansion of knowledge that is at fault. The discoveries of the natural sciences and their applications can work, and have worked, to the betterment of humankind and society. What should trouble us, however, is the extent to which these advances have been accompanied by diminishing respect for human life itself and for the dignity of the person. The ability to produce a fertilized ovum in a test tube and help it develop into a living child is a great accomplishment, but should not be allowed to reduce the creation of new life to nothing more than a bio-chemical process as our contemporary advocates of abortion too often contend. It is no accident that the immorality of "sex when desired" has opened the way to the immorality of "abortion on demand" so that the intentional and instrumental destruction of human life is often dismissed as the simple removal of "an inch of tissue" or "the products of conception."

Consider in this light Arnold's chapter on the heart. To him this is the true center of *Innenland*, the source of all true joy and all great thoughts, the foundation of all intentions and wishes. What are we to make of this? A generation so firmly locked into a purely physicalist view of human nature and behavior is not all that likely to share Arnold's more exalted conceptualization of the "Heart" and its meaning. The "miracles" of surgical technology have taken precedence over the more traditional miracles of divine origin. The human heart, first made transferable and now made replaceable by a mechanical device or the heart of some lesser animal order, is simply "not that big a deal" anymore.

Of course, this is not at all what he meant to convey. Certainly a man of his great learning was familiar enough with the heart in its anatomical structure and function as a muscle, a pump. The "Heart" of which he spoke was something much different.

To borrow from the lyric of a once-popular song, the Heart he had in mind was the kind of "heart" the manager of a hopelessly outclassed baseball team told his players they "gotta have."

In this sense, the heart as source of motivation and commitment is still familiar enough, however much scientific and technological progress may have diminished its force and credibility as symbol. Therefore, what Arnold intends to say still retains much of its relevance and force. However, to make his point most effectively today and to reach those who need his message, he would probably find it necessary to modify or lessen the scope of some of his generalizations and put that message in a less salvational context.

Please do not misunderstand. Whatever changes in approach he might make, were he here to undertake a new revision of this most significant work, he would not feel the slightest need to change the substance or the dynamic thrust of his message. And we can be sure that just as that message was found incompatible with the aims and objectives of the Nazi "New Order," so would it be found incompatible with the attitudes and policies prevailing in the United States today. It might not be necessary to bury the pages in expectation of some imminent diaspora, perhaps, but—assuming the message were heard and put into practice—it would probably be viewed as dangerous, even subversive, doctrine.

"In such agitated times as ours today, the Enemy of our soul has a powerful band of accomplices that want to shatter and destroy it." The "agitated times" of which he wrote were the

1930's. If anything, the passage of a half-century has left the situation more threatening than it was then. Now the Enemy and his "band of accomplices" have the power to destroy the planet and all who live upon it. The "madman" who set out to restore Germany to its "place in the sun" has been replaced by "sane" men who, no less chauvinistic in spirit, declare their determination to make certain their nation becomes, or remains, Number One. And they are prepared to preside over the slaughter of tens of millions of human beings to achieve that goal!

"But whoever kills man lays violent hands on the countenance of God. He commits a sacrilege against the task of the Spirit. . . . When men cooperate with every breath of God's Spirit, it becomes impossible for them to fight with murderous intent and kill each other." How can one reconcile that vision with today's reality which finds our own and other societies organized in almost total cooperation to kill and destroy on a scale Arnold would have found it impossible to imagine?

The answer, of course, is that one can't. The vision has been abandoned, even by most professed Christians, in a mad pursuit of security through power. It is well, then, to have this voice from the past—a voice from the time when the greatest horror until now was being readied—call us back to the vision.

The situation is not altogether hopeless, I am happy to say. One of the greatest benefits I have gained from my work in the peace movement has been the joy of working with young people who are commited to peace, non-violence, and social justice. Not all of them speak Arnold's language. In place of his intensity of biblical spirituality one is more likely to find a more pragmatic sense of outrage against injustice and compassion toward its victims. Even those whose involvement is primarily spiritual in origin are likely to give direct action preference over extended theological analysis or exhortation. Yet, they would understand what Arnold is saying because the essentials of the vision which was his are also theirs.

The Kingdom of God, Scripture tells us, is within us. It is passing strange that in his analysis of *Innenland* Arnold does not rely more heavily on this particular assurance. Not specifically, that is. One cannot read these intensely spiritual pages without knowing that there, in that interior space which is the core of each individual being, is where the confrontation with God takes place and the decisions to serve him or not are made.

Scripture has another word for us. We are called to be at peace with all men "so far as it lies" within *us*. This may not always be possible, Paul suggests, but living in peace with others is not to be determined by what they do, or threaten to do; rather, the test is the extent of our own desire or determination to live at peace with everyone. That, too, is a decision that must ultimately be made in the most intimate and hidden recesses of our *Innenland*.

As a testament of faith, then—of a faith hardened in the crucible of sacrifice and the anticipation of even greater sacrifices yet to be made—this little volume commands the attention and respectful consideration of everyone concerned about the role of the Christian in the modern world. It may not provide all the answers we need, and some of the answers may not be those we seek or are ready to accept. Nevertheless, in this context reservations fade and differences in perspective become inconsequential.

The intensity of Arnold's spiritual commitment breaks through all barriers of style to lend credibility to his affirmations and explanations which, without that fervor to sustain them, could easily be put aside as overstated pieties and platitudes. Even those who, like myself, might not be ready to take his teachings fully to heart or prepared to adapt our lifestyle to the Bruderhof model will find themselves challenged to reassess the values which govern our daily lives and behavior. After all, we *are* living at the moment when it becomes ever clearer that "the mystery of iniquity" is at work among us. It is well that at such a time we are called upon to contemplate who we are and what we have become, as well as where we should be heading. This little book provides the occasion for such self-study and provides some of the guideposts along the way to that uncharted *Innenland* where each of us in the solitude of that private space can confront God and learn what he asks of us.

*Gordon Zahn*

# THE INNER LIFE

In the first decades of this century, it was the will to power that asserted itself in the most diverse forms. It ensnared men in the bustle of outer activity and used up all their energy to increase material possessions. Today again it is the will to brutal self-assertion and ruthless power expansion that lashes our nation and other nations like a raging tempest. This gives a new impetus not only to national independence and to providing work for the unemployed; it also gives a new impetus to collective self-will and personal property and ousts everything else. With increasing unrestraint, the will to live our own life as a nation or as an individual lays claim on our whole being for the upkeep and improvement of our material existence; it is not able to provide a deep inner foundation. On the other hand, a will for the innermost life and for the all-commanding power of God's Kingdom as love and justice—a will for God—forces us into an inner detachment. In this detachment, the solitariness of the soul with God should become a community of two, and then, with His Church, become a community of many.

This is why Eckhart (who in many ways knew the inner life as few others have done) said: "Nowhere is there perfect peace save in the detached heart. Therefore God would rather be there than in any other being or in any other virtue."[1] This saying, however, is true only when detachment is a separation from the unfruitful and dead works of darkness, when it leads to the living building-up of the City of Light. In this City of Light, the nature of the Kingdom of God will be revealed to everyone as unity in all the diligence and courage of the loving works of community. Wherever God is, His Kingdom—the final Kingdom—draws near. He is the God of Peace, whose presence brings freedom from all inner restlessness, all dividedness of heart, and every hostile impulse. However, Eckhart forgets all too easily that the Living God is action just as much as He is peace. His peace is indeed the deepest unity of heart, the harmonious accord of the great diversity of all the gifts and powers of the soul. But on this foundation He brings into being as the goal of His creation an outer unity of all action, a unity that rejoices in every object of love, brings justice into operation for all men, and builds a material world that makes peace a reality on every front through the Holy Spirit. God wants to bestow an indestructible harmony upon man's inner life, a harmony that shall have an effect

[1] Meister Johannes Eckhart, c. 1260–c. 1327.

outwardly in mighty melodies of love. Power to act
is what results from the energy born of inner gathering. When hearts are gathered, it leads to the
gathering of a people who show in their industrious
work that the Kingdom of God is justice, peace, and
joy in the Holy Spirit.

With respect to this life-task—this call from
Christ—it is important to emphasize once more today
that our capacity for work is sure to become exhausted
and mechanical, yes, our strength will be sapped at
the core if no deepening is given to the inner life in
stillness and quiet. As soon as inner quiet is lost, the
holy springs of the inner world that bring life-giving
water to our spiritual life must fail at the very source.
Like a man dying of thirst, the overburdened man of
today longs for his inner life to be strengthened and
quickened because he feels how miserably he will die
otherwise. The inner strength that comes from the
Source and in tranquil silence lets God himself speak
and act, leads the believers away from sinking in
death to rising in life, to a life that flows outward in
streams of creative spirit, without losing itself in externals. This strength as "active stillness" leads believers to work for the world in such a way that they do
not become "worldly," and yet they never become
inactive.

These are times of distress; they do not allow us
to retreat just because we are willfully blind to the
overwhelming urgency of the tasks that press upon
human society. We cannot look for inner detachment

in an inner and outer isolation, as implied by Eckhart's sayings (which are liable to be misunderstood, to say the least). We are thankful that the highly mechanized nature of world economics today does not allow this pious selfishness anymore, for it gives us more protection from self-deception than we had in earlier times. But the lack of vital and effective action shows us when our striving after detachment has not penetrated to the inmost springs of creative power. Where this power is at work in man, there is a detachment which is a thorough letting-go of self and therefore a freedom for the hardest work; this gathers believing people into the most living kind of community. Their love to all men now presses forward out of all isolation to the ends of the earth, and yet they will never be able to give up the common gathering at the focal point of strength.

To the man who is responsible in his conscience, the only thing that could justify withdrawing into his inner self to escape today's confusing, hectic whirl would be that his fruitfulness is enriched by it. It is a question of gaining within, through unity with the eternal powers, that strength of character which is ready to be tested in the stream of the world, the strength that alone can cope with the demands of this age. Not flight, but gathering for attack, is the watchword. We must never withdraw from the rushing stream of present-day life into a selfishness of soul that makes our love grow cold in the face of need and the countless paths of guilt connected with it.

Our detachment, turned into coldness of heart, would then reach such a height of injustice that it would exceed the injustice of the world. Unless we share the distress and guilt of the world, we fall prey to untruthfulness and lifelessness, to eternal and temporal death. And anyone who is prepared to share only the inner need of his fellowmen, and not their outer need as well, fully and completely, is cutting life into halves. Thereby he is losing the inner half of life, the very part he was supposed to be gaining or preserving. For he has forgotten Jesus Christ, who took on outer need just as much as inner need: in His eyes the two are inseparably *one*. It is possible to share lovingly and militantly in the life of our times only when we respond with every fiber of our being to the work demanded, when in every drop of our heart's blood we feel the distress, want to share in suffering it, and thereby in actively overcoming it. It is in quietness that we find the way to give this help.

Jean Paul describes a raging tempest in which the surface of the water is broken up in jagged and foaming confusion while the sun still shines on it, without being hidden by turbulent clouds.[1] The mirror of our feelings also cannot help becoming stormy and agitated sometimes with all the seething activity in which we are obliged to live and carry on our work. Yet our hearts know of a Heaven with a Sun which in radiant quiet preserves an untouched and

[1] Pseudonym for Jean Paul Friedrich Richter, 1763–1825.

inviolable strength. This Heaven is the rising Sun of God's approaching reign. Jesus Christ, the Morning Star of the future, not only proclaimed it to us; He also brought it close to us all in His life and death, in His word and deed. The following words of Fichte will be understood by anyone who sees this Heaven: "Do you wish to see God face to face as He himself is? Do not look for Him beyond the clouds; you can find Him everywhere, wherever you are." The Kingdom of God draws near over all the earth. God is near wherever a complete reversal of all things is sought—the reversal that brings His rule with it. His Kingdom has no territorial boundaries.

We are not Christians (in the only sense in which it is possible to be Christians—in the inner sense that affects all outward things as well) until we have experienced in our own hearts these decisive words about the presence of Christ:

> The righteousness based on faith says, Do not say in your heart, "Who will ascend into heaven?" (that is, to bring Christ down) or "Who will descend into the abyss?" (that is, to bring Christ up from the dead). But what does it say? The word is near you, on your lips and in your heart.
>
> (Romans 10:6–8, RSV)

The Word comes into man's heart because it has come into the world. The eternal Word became temporal flesh; God's Son became the Son of Man. Every time what you do is done sincerely, believed whole-heartedly, and confessed openly, the Word becomes again body and flesh in your mouth, in your heart, in the work of the believing Church, in the loving, active community which is its organism. It is through the Holy Spirit that this comes about, just as it did when the Son came for the first time. In order to penetrate the life of man, the Word goes to his inmost heart again and again. The Kingdom has no time boundaries.

No eye can see light apart from itself, but only in itself. Light comes from outside, and its rays illuminate the inside. God's Morning Star and His Rising Sun draw near to us from the Other World. When we believe this fact and when this news reaches our inmost life, the Morning Star has arisen in our hearts. We are filled with light because the Light of the World has reached us from afar. So it gives light to every man who comes into this world. Seeing takes place only when the eye receives light-rays in its own deepest depths. "Therefore you cannot grasp God apart from yourself. He Himself must let the rays of His Spirit pierce deep into the depths of your heart to stamp His image there in order that you may know Him." In Jesus, the image of God has appeared so clearly and so undeniably that from now on it is from Him that we receive man's calling into our hearts. The image of God that Jesus brings to us is love: love as the will to unity. We are called to be images of God, and through this calling His Spirit wants to rule all men and all things and form them into one united whole. The Kingdom has no subjective boundaries.

We see God directly before our inmost heart as soon as the light is no longer eclipsed by all the busyness of our ego as it obstinately pushes its way to the fore. God shows Himself to us as the beaming sun that alone can bring abiding life. He brings in the new day, which as His day brings judgment on the dark life of self. He seeks to bring all men into redeeming light and unite them under His rulership. We find the focal point of our inner life in God, the central Sun of our existence, because in Him we recognize the central fire of all creation, of history, and of the history of the last things. Without Him, collectedness of spirit in the depths of our soul will be cast to the winds again and again. Only through our becoming one with God in the depths of our being will it become possible. A battle can be won only when the field marshal and his staff keep completely calm in the midst of all the turmoil. Similarly, each of us is able to cope with the demands of today's need and distress only when he has found an inner collectedness in God. And we shall find this only when lightning from the Kingdom of God has struck and lit up the whole horizon.

Every bit of life must have a center somewhere deep inside it. Just as the earth without its glowing center would be no less dead than the moon, just as the inner core contains the life-strength of the fruit, just as a flower's beautiful petal-cups shield the organs of fertilization, in the same way there can be only *one* center for all life-energy: the hidden and the inner. The power of God's Kingdom lies hidden in its innermost core, in the heart of God. It comes to light in Jesus, the hidden focus of all history. Jesus reveals this power at the very heart of faith to the simple and to children. It remains hidden from the wise and clever because only the childlike heart is able to grasp the plan of love. The only way our soul can know God and be known by Him is for us to become one in our own inner depths with the center of all worlds and all life in them. The inmost core decides between life and death.

Therefore, the most dangerous sickening of life does not halt at the external forms of life but proceeds with its decay and destruction to attack the innermost core. In fact, life could not really be affected by sickness if the core of our being were to remain untouched by it. We are sick, and we do fall prey to death, because we have become estranged from the fire that is the core of all life, the core of all that takes place. In this state of sickness we understand nothing of God's judgment in His history. Through this sickening, our inner eye is blinded so that it cannot see the Kingdom of God. Every weakening of inwardness strikes at the source of our life-power. Every strengthening of our outward existence that is won at the expense of inwardness squanders our vital strength and endangers our inner existence. Only wealth of life gathered in the innermost depths makes us capable of that quality of generosity which finds its happiness in giving. The innermost core of God's Kingdom is the surrendering love and active sacrifice of the pure life.

In the same way, it is in the innermost core of our life that the love of the sacrificed Christ kindles the rich fire of renunciation, a letting-go and surrendering of everything that is given us in the way of personal abilities and possessions. Every impoverishment and sickening of our inner being means a loss of warmth and depth, a loss that shows up plainly in all our efforts and activities. Every healing of the inner life leads to loving sacrifice, that is, to purer and more vigorous action. Jesus has wielded the sword of speech more powerfully than any other man against the danger that religion, man's inmost treasure, becomes superficial. No one has stressed more than He did the vital importance of the actual state of a man's inner life. Because He is the Heart of God, He brought the Kingdom of God, and this Kingdom seeks to gain authority over all things by touching hearts and changing everything, starting with the heart. That is why He seeks the inner life of all men. We know from Him that even the most untruthful man, even the man who is farthest from God, has an inner being. God seeks with all the means of judgment and love to move the heart of each man: He wants the approach of His day, just as much as the effect of His love, to bring each one to look in his own heart and turn around. In this way, everything will be changed by being overthrown and set up new. And He sees our hearts as they are. All purifying or whitewashing of externals is in vain. "Inwardly you are full of hypocrisy and lawlessness." "Inwardly they are full of greed and self-indulgence, full of dead men's bones and all kinds of rottenness." Jesus hates the outward appearance of piety and holiness when the heart dishonestly boasts of spiritual values it does not possess and sinks further and further away from God. He Himself said the most serious thing that can be said about this: "This people draws near to me with their mouth and honors me with their lips, but their hearts are far removed from me. But they serve me in vain because they teach teachings that are nothing but the commandments of men."

As a result of the wars in this century and all the consequent shocks and breakdowns, men should feel that God wants to use the heavy burden of our times to bring them to examine themselves. Again it is all-important that it is not with our mouth only that we promise to change and not with our lips only that we honor the Ruler to whom alone all power is given. The will of the heart must be turned into deed if it is serious and sincere. Sincerity is decisive. God wants through the judgment of His earnest love to bring about a real transformation in all men who are ready for it—a change of heart, a change in actual inner condition, and with that a change in their whole attitude to life.

And what glimpses into the dark recesses of man's heart have been afforded by war and its savagery! Fear for existence, greed to possess, nationalistic fervor, and revolutionary passions—all these are stirred up by war and continue to work on and on. Our times have once more revealed the state of man's inner life: he is filled with everything but God, who alone fulfills man's destiny. And yet we still deceive ourselves.

People speak of dedication and sacrifice of life— their devotion unto death for the sake of brothers, friends, comrades, the homeland, freedom, or justice. What they mean by all this is the killing and plundering of all those they look upon as enemies of these things so precious to them. Just this is what makes Jesus give such a strong warning about those who come in sheep's clothing, "but inwardly they are ravening wolves"! Their hearts are set on plunder and destruction because the essence of sin—unbroken self-seeking—rules in them as much as ever in spite of all Christian disguises and in spite of all quasi-prophetic banners of justice. The condition of any war-torn nation and the subsequent opportunities for power politics expose in an appalling way the gruesome violence with which man's inner being is filled. Truly, man's condition today appears just as in the words of the Psalm on which the Letter to the Romans throws so serious a light: "Their heart is destruction," destruction that we prepare for ourselves and others.

Like the fate of the countries devastated by war, man's inner being today can be compared to a deep mountain ravine: dark shadows of judgment are spread over it. Only withered trunks and bony roots betray to a discerning eye the fact that death did not always rule here. The water that used to be the life of this valley has been blocked. Stones and boulders fill the ravine and seem to have buried every hope. The deeper and more truthfully man sees into the actual condition of his inner life, the more hopeless and desperate his fate seems to him. What amazement must have filled the Samaritan woman when the infallible mouth of the Messiah declared that her buried inner life was to be completely renewed and filled forever with fresh strength and rich content! There is a life-giving water that today too transforms the darkest abyss or the most awful desolation into a place of joy and surging life. It is the Spirit of Him who said: "The water I shall give him will become in him a spring of water welling up to eternal life." From this deepest of all springs even the uttermost devastation that has come upon lands and peoples shall be transformed everywhere into a region and people filled with far-reaching peace, a place where the powers of God's future world shall be poured out through the Holy Spirit.

God does not want our inner self to remain bleak and desolate—a dark abyss. He is able to change the storms of His judgment, which threaten the terrified soul, into the sunshine of undeserved love. He wants to bring peace and clarity to the heart where until now disruption and darkness have reigned. God's Day of Judgment threatens to smash conquered and unconquered nations alike, yes, the entire mammonistic world economy. But once we renounce the kingdom of Mammon and murder and lying and impurity in order to belong from then on to the Kingdom of God, His Day of Judgment, the Day of the Lord, will become the Day of *Salvation.*

God knows of the inner fight: how it goes on with deep pain in the hidden recesses of the heart. He knows that the conscience lives there, bringing its witness again and again to the heart's awareness. He knows the hidden thoughts, how they accuse and excuse each other. He knows how many a one wrestles in vain with inner ties that bind him to what is base. He knows with what lying power false demonic ideals and idols try to assert themselves. He knows that the ravening beast of prey confuses the conscience in the guise of an angel of light and so-called liberation.

The inward man delights in God's Law. He would so gladly live according to it. At the same time, along with the demands made by God's justice, other claims stir his inmost being—the claims of his own life, of his nation, or of the oppressed classes. He would like to be free for God's justice in both the inner life and the outer circumstances. And he cannot. The Spirit draws him toward the heavenly City of God's Church and God's Kingdom. But he is bound by the heavy weight of the iron-fisted autonomy of those other

things—bound to the earthly cities of human community and human sovereignty and their bloody interests.
God knows that all nations and all men live in this
inner struggle. For God has written the Book of the
Law on the hearts of even the remotest nations. He
alone, and whoever is in unity with Him in the all-
discerning Spirit, can judge and discern the hidden
depths of man. The Father sees into what is hidden.
He delights in the truth that is within the heart. He
wants to teach us to know the truth in the hidden
depths, in the innermost recesses of the heart. And
only God's pure truth in His perfect love, as it took
shape in Jesus and His first Church, has the power
to set us free. Everything else is lying and deceit.

The fate of the countries so hard hit today brings
to mind a remarkable story about a remote, parched
valley, whose impoverished inhabitants vaguely re-
membered a time when it had been different and
better. Once upon a time, a life-giving mountain
stream had flowed there and brought wealth and
happiness to the valley. But guilt, in which all who
lived there had a share, had ruined everything; the
great mountains began to move. Huge boulders
plunged into the valley. It seemed as though absolutely everything was about to be buried under the
debris. Neither buildings nor rows of houses were any
protection. Then the hurtling masses of rock stopped.
They halted in front of the houses. But the river
was blocked. The life that had flourished seemed
destroyed forever. Poverty and distress began their

rule. Even memories of the past began to fade slowly away.

But a son of the valley grew up, despised by the others, who was moved by the fate of his people. Day and night he thought about delivering them, ready to attempt it. He knew about the stream and where it was blocked. He accomplished the colossal task, moving the mountainous weight of rocks; but as he moved the last boulder, letting the water flow once more into the valley, he, the savior of his people, was buried under it. Yet he rose to life again, this man who had risked his life for their sake. He ruled forevermore over his people, who had had everything given back to them.

It is Jesus who has moved the boulder of our mountainously heavy guilt so that the river of life can flow unhindered into our inner being. As Lord over our innermost being, Jesus brings riches and happiness to our inner life. And just as He healed the bodies of the sick and possessed, also now in this relentless catastrophe of world history He wants to set free the buried bodies and ruined workplaces and make a new life possible in His land. Our hearts cannot be set free from the deadening pressure of hidden sin until His liberating action, given as His gift, gains room in our innermost being. And when this experience has become ours, the essential thing is to allow Him to take command and have more and more authority.

When His Kingdom comes to us in this way, we live from within according to the spiritual laws of His Kingdom, also in our work and in the communal order of our life. Even the outer shape of our life shall be in accord with the Kingdom of God as His prophets portrayed it. When His Word rules in us, when His nature unfolds in us, it is wealth of life undreamed of, which floods the parched depths of our inner being and pours forth from there into the world outside as living, active love. In place of the cloud of judgment that threatens everything, comes the superabundant light of His revelation. This light shows the living way. The Church of faith and love already gains today the possibility of judging and ordering the innermost as well as the outermost details of life according to the justice, peace, and joy of His Kingdom.

In this light, the somber darkness of war with all its causes and consequences is revealed as that guilt which in many people causes the river of life to be blocked. To forget that Jesus is Life becomes widespread. Because men seek their life in other waters, it is inevitable that everything becomes blocked and buried. God lets war come over nations like a heavy landslide because it is His will to give inner help through such radical intervention. But it turns out as the Revelation of John foretold about the last times: "And those that remained, who were not killed by these plagues, still did not repent of the work of their hands. Neither did they repent of their manifold murders. Indeed, they blasphemed God in Heaven instead of repenting of their deeds."

Untold numbers turn sharply away from the way of Jesus. They seek out the way of idols so that they can continue to worship Mammon all the more zealously—Mammon, the Murderer from the Beginning, the Father of Lies, the Prince of Impure Spirits. They endeavor to make themselves strong through impure streams of racial ties instead of at long last looking for the one pure Spring. Through collapse on all sides, we are directed more earnestly than ever before to the One who took upon Himself our poverty and distress to make us pure and strong in His Spirit. Every single person should have recognized at long last that no human, self-made effort can bring peace and life to the earth. Only the sovereign reign of God can do this. In the midst of the serious situation today, God himself wants to be the Savior and Helper in our inner life and in every area of our life. There is only one Gospel for all creation, only one and the same Gospel for all nations, for every class of people, and for everybody's homeland. Whoever represents a different gospel for himself, his nation, or his class brings a curse with him.

The reality of God is proved by the fact that He brings about the renewal and strengthening for our hearts that we cannot find without Him. The unity of Jesus with the Father is the living reality of His divine Sonship and the same as the unity of God and

Christ with the Holy Spirit. This unity shows itself in our innermost life. For there His Spirit works the powerful religious and moral transformation that could never be attained without Him. He is unity in Himself and in us. Therefore His Spirit can represent and spread only unity and peace, also in outer life. He knows of only One way and One leadership. Jesus Christ, who is Lord and Spirit, goes no roundabout way and knows no separate mediator.

God gives Himself in the certainty of direct contact. In Him alone does the heart's need for security find the firm ground of the here and now, for which it must long continually. The presence of Christ is the wonderful gift of God in which we receive perfect unity with God in love and faith. Through this experience, however, the stark difference between His purity and our guilt dawns on us just as powerfully. We stand in the midst of disunity between men, classes, and nations, while He is and remains unity. It is precisely in this complete oneness that we become aware of the abysmal difference that separates our nature from His.

The writings of the apostles call this experience the illumination of our hearts by God. It brings the brightness of His glory into our inner being. God shines in Christ and in His countenance. Illuminated by the presence of God, the hidden recesses of the heart are revealed, so that we have to cast ourselves down and worship Him. What overpowers us is the fact that the light of His incomprehensibly glorious nature makes us feel all the more deeply the darkness of our own being. If we accept the life of Jesus with His unmistakable words and deeds, if we accept them unadulterated and without any devious interpretations, our entire life, private and public, will be revealed as utterly opposed and hostile to Him.

Only in Jesus can the inner part of man find happiness and inmost satisfaction: nothing else corresponds to what our innermost being is and should be, in the light of its origin. Only when our life is hidden with Christ in God do we experience our real, unique destiny, which without Him has to remain buried in the dark. This destiny is to be God's image: to rule in His Spirit over everything through love and love's creative power. The more we experience His wealth of life, the more we long with all our heart to grow in this inner experience and this creative shaping of life. For the experience of God's gifts and the knowledge of His divine rulership over everything can never reach a conclusion in this life. It needs to be renewed every day.

The great commotion in the world of today makes it more and more urgent to gain inner strength in quiet encounter with Christ. This will make it possible for us to remain under the rule of His authority. Since we are situated in the midst of a world so terribly unpeaceful, we need constant nourishment for our inner life. It is important to look toward and think about that which is above external things and in direct contrast to the outward form they take today.

Instead of following the weak and alien spirits of hate and of violence, of lying and of impure, greedy possessiveness, we are allowed to follow the one Spirit who alone is stronger than all other spirits. Only the strongest power of inner resistance can prevent our inner life from being buried by what is happening around us now on the earth.

Without a rebirth in our hearts, we will glean from fluctuating world events either a false meaning—based perhaps only on material considerations or on emotional or racial ties—or no meaning at all. The course of history is interpreted falsely by very many people in the interests of their own nation, for example, or their own society. For most people, though, it never has any meaning at all. There is only *one* possible way of bringing this confusion to an end. Man as a whole and the whole of his life must undergo a complete about-turn toward the Kingdom of God. Rebirth is the only name we can give to such a radical change with its childlike trust in God's intervention and firm, manly expectation of it. This is the complete opposite of the former life. It is only through such a complete change that we—by going through judgment—can recognize in all that happens the approach and intervention of God's rule. We can never see the Kingdom of God or have any part in it without a rebirth of heart that breaks down the whole structure of our life and then makes a new start, a completely different one. Only a new beginning that starts from the very bottom in the process of becoming a true man, only the rebirth that starts at the very beginning, is able to prepare us for the Kingdom of God. It must be a new beginning of our whole personal life.

Consequently, it is only through the Spirit who embraces all the powers of the future Kingdom of God that this can happen. Only the Spirit of the Kingdom of God can put a seal on the passport without which the door into this Kingdom remains shut— the passport to God's Kingdom, which is meant to confirm that we already live now in the Spirit and in the order of the final Kingdom. But just as a tiny, newborn baby is far from being able to master life, so too the rebirth brought about by the Holy Spirit is neither more nor less than the beginning of new life, which still needs to be strengthened and completed. For us weak men, however, this is possible only as a slow process of being made fit for God's Kingdom and His righteousness. Even after rebirth has given the first glimpse into the Kingdom of God, our hearts still remain subject to the old inhibitions and restrictions epitomized as "flesh" by Paul, that methodical thinker of early Christian times. He testified of himself explicitly that his flesh had no peace, not only because of struggles from without but just as much because of fears from within.

What is incomplete in our existence gives the believer a powerful incentive to deepen his inner life constantly. It is of the utmost importance that in these serious and extremely menacing days we gain a growing clarity about our inner life. We must not let our emotional nature deceive our hearts in these agitated times. Even when it has been touched by the Holy Spirit, our excitable inner nature remains weak. Our hearts are flooded as the blood circulates; our emotional life flows in this bloodstream and often continues as long as we live to be determined by its urges and feelings.

Should our blood be gripped and swept along by the excitement in all those around us, we often fall prey to it entirely because we are not able to put up a true resistance born of the Spirit. The distress of our own class or our own nation has a particularly strong effect on us. Mass suggestion used by great national movements appeals to our blood ties and class solidarity and often works so decisively on us that we utterly forget the call to the Kingdom of God and His Spirit, or we completely falsify it. Even if we continue to profess Him, emotional ties and fear for existence have driven the Spirit away from us. In order to face all fears, and still more, in order to resist all the impure and bloody "raptures" of fanaticism, our consciences need a healing that steadily gains ground. This healing can come about solely through the holy, all-loving, utterly pure, and completely true Spirit, the Spirit of Jesus Christ, who unites all good in Himself. His objectivity is sober and clear.

No experience, however agitating, and no shock, however violent or bitter, must be allowed to sweep past without this result: that the rule of Christ in us gains ground in our heart and in our whole life. The aim of His rule is to fill our inner life with an objective clarity that cannot be shattered by any force of circumstance. His Word and His Spirit want to work in us uninterruptedly as His instruments in order to make us strong in every battle and capable of the hardest work. The blessing of all good shall conduct us so firmly and clearly on the way of Jesus Christ—the way that leads straight ahead—that neither successes nor failures in the world can make us swerve into false ways.

We have to follow the same way as Jesus; we must follow it just as Jesus did. Then no seductive call will divert us from this mission, which He left to us as His mission. In just the same way as the Father sent Him into the world, He sends us: in just the same way, with the same stand in life, completely free from adulteration by other elements! Only in this way will our life be fruitful. He wants all our gifts to come to life and unfold in order to equip us for the new tasks of the changing world situation. The rulership of Christ denotes strength for the inner life through inner gathering and consecration, and through this, through this alone, also strength for an outer life with a living influence in the right work or occupation.

To become strong in our inner being can mean only one thing: that Christ lives in our hearts through faith because we are being grounded and rooted in love. We need Christ all the time in our inner being, the Christ who was crucified for us, the Christ who is alive for us. He invades us with His fullness, with all the fullness of God, which wants to pour itself over all spheres of our activity as the supreme authority of love. God is love. Only he who remains in love remains in God and God in him. God's rulership is the Kingdom of love. Love is His justice. Because His Kingdom knows no frontiers, His Messiah-King has put the love of God to friend and foe into our hearts. It is poured into our hearts through the Holy Spirit.

Whoever betrays this by shutting out love to his opponents or to enemies of his class or nation drives away the Holy Spirit and delivers up his heart to deceptive spirits. Love wants to flood our private as well as our public life and rule over it in such a way that there can be no rival authority. Paul prays for this for all men because it is the true and the only strengthening for man's inner being. In our inner life we need an experience of Christ that transcends all knowledge. This means that as King of the final Kingdom He rules over our lives already here and now in exactly the same way as He will in His final Kingdom.

We need men of prayer who, like Paul, bend their knees and lift hands that are unstained with blood or any kind of impurity so that through the Spirit of God the believers may be strengthened powerfully in their inmost being—strengthened in their whole attitude to life. We need to be reminded daily that the inner man must be renewed from day to day even if the outer man, the body, perishes in hunger, distress, and misery or is carried off and destroyed by persecution and death for the sake of truth. If in the storm of public opinion and the towering waves of chaos, we want to keep a clear, firm course instead of inwardly suffering shipwreck—then our hidden inner being needs daily the quiet haven of communion with God.

# THE HEART

World war or world crisis is a time of sharp testing and deep affliction. It tests our endurance to its very limits, bringing in its train loss of national wealth and disruption of world economy, unemployment and impoverishment, mutual hostility, and untold ills that shatter public confidence. Even the most indifferent must feel that it depends on what his heart is able to bear whether he will pass the test or not. Men who had nothing but a smile for demands made by the inner life then feel how important it is that their hearts are firm. The faithfulness of true community, like the faithfulness of the individual, denotes the heart's energy to hold all good powers together and to ward off all destructive ones. We need the inmost strength of stout hearts in order to be able to bear the consequences of war or world crisis without permanent injury.

Suffering is an appeal to our hearts. It forces us to be on the watch for ways of finding the necessary strength and courage. For the heart affects the whole of man. Being the inmost core, the heart means more than anything else not only for the spirit, but just as much for the body. Even physical capacity depends on strength of heart. No feeling, thought, or motion of the will is without influence on the body. "Even in the human body, the heart counts more than the hand; the strength that gives the body life is in the heart." Ovid recognized this even in those early days. Man's life radiates from his heart and preserves the center of its strength in this innermost core. The outer man perishes. The heart decides between life and death. For it is so closely linked with the soul and is meant to be so open to the spirit that it can and should have everlasting life.

People who are guided by superficialities cannot stand up to any hard trial. They have too feeble a concept of what wealth of life and strength can fill the heart. The most important things in life are lost to them. Only events that have a powerful outer effect give them some idea of what power the inner life can have. The great wide mouth of a mighty river once showed Columbus what riches must lie hidden in the interior behind the newly discovered coast. This coast could not possibly be mistaken any longer for the edge of a small island. And no one could possibly remain indifferent to the heart of a continent! The sun that shone over it was indeed familiar. Clouds could indeed be seen gathering over it. No one could from then on be satisfied with the outside edge, however—the beach strewn with shells and wreckage and pounded monotonously by the sea of the world outside. The discoverers could not rest until the unfathomable wealth of the interior lay before their astonished eyes.

The whole world shall recognize, by the stream of light radiating from the seven lampstands, what a land of light, what a part of God's Kingdom is given to the Church of Jesus Christ. The City of God as the City on the Hill shall be visible to all lands far and wide so that all seeking people may have a longing to know the center of its inner life, the inner secret of its free citizenship and its Church unity. All men over all the earth shall ask about the citizenship of the Kingdom of God, about His Embassy here and now, and about the future order it represents. They must recognize one thing above all, that they must become one with the heart of this Church and City of God before they can enter its gates.

The most recent world history shows us that neither foreign rule nor home rule will come to any good unless the heart of a country is won. For all wealth lies hidden within. Whoever does not learn to understand the heart of God in Jesus Christ, whoever will not begin to journey through all the outlying regions of God's world rule to the very center in order to become one with the ultimate will of God's heart, whoever does not seek the Holy of Holies, will never understand that God wants only one thing. He will never understand that in spite of the fact that in history God has appointed a bloody, diplomatic world government anchored in the right to property, God wants only *one* thing in the end: love without violence, freedom from all possessions and property rights, simple truthfulness and brotherly justice, community of all men with all men without self-interest and property—that is, the Kingdom and the Church.

Whoever keeps his back turned on the heart of God will be just as perplexed when confronted by the mystery of the human heart. For that is where the likeness of God shall be revealed. Such a man will never be able to grasp

> The greatest wonder in all creation,
> Of time and space the masterpiece:
> The heart of man with its elation,
> The heart with all its ecstasies.

The Bible, which speaks of the heart in such a rich and profound way, is of all books the only one that can satisfy the inner man and fill the heart. If it is not seen superficially according to its letter but deeply in its heart and soul, it witnesses everywhere to the heart as the innermost mystery. It even goes so far as using the Hebrew expressions for "heart" and for "that which is within" as synonyms. In the Bible the heart is the antithesis of superficiality and pretense. What penetrates to the inmost depths does not simply stay on the surface. What comes from the inmost depths is the noblest and sincerest of all. If a man's heart is corrupt, nothing he touches remains incorrupt. But the outer life resists the inner life and strives against it. Only seldom is there harmony between them.

A pure, creative spirit expresses what is within very clearly and intelligibly by outward and visible signs. An impure and untruthful spirit, on the other hand, misuses the outward expression to falsify the true state of affairs. Then the outward appearance is only there to hide what is within, as public economy and politics reveal so painfully in war and in peace. We in our days have had to look on with horror while spirits who have fallen prey to hate and hostility, of whatever party or nation, have practiced the most hateful misuse of the spoken, written, and printed word. They all, every one of them, practice it to this day, dishonestly exaggerating and inventing failures and mistakes in the enemy's camp, and, just as much, exaggerating and inventing advantages and elements of truth in the home camp. Every honest man must be warned of the daily flood of printed matter that bears down on him: *Cave canem*! Here you will get barked at and bitten; there is no sense, no understanding, and no insight here because there is no justice. Pass by! Words desecrate the truth! Here the heart is cloaked in lies.

In the Scriptures, the heart is called that part of man which is hidden in his inner being. The thought is even intensified by terms like the "inmost" heart and the "depths" of the heart. The secrets of the heart are known to the Scriptures. In the Scriptures, anyone is marked as unhappy who has to hide himself in an armor of lies and dishonesty because he wants to appear different from what he truly is. Whoever gets entangled in hypocrisy and deceit cannot open up and pour out his heart even before God—the very One who wants to make the heart glad because He loves it and because He wants to give it truth and genuineness.

Ultimately however, no one can hide his innermost being, for man must *do* what is in his heart. And even if he does not want to admit it, his *deeds* will finally reveal whether his heart is right or wrong. The surprises in this direction that war and postwar times have brought for many should be stamped on our hearts as unforgettable warnings. We must not be indifferent to the abysses that have yawned in front of us: impure and unbridled passions, boundless lies and deceptions, the unrestrained fury of murder and looting, the loveless triumph of ruthless profiteering, the renewed increase of social injustice and oppressions, and the deception of class hatred and racism! All of that, and still more, breaks out with the most fearsome violence in war and in the revolution and violent repression that follow it, in inflation, and in the heated political opinions that excite nearly everybody. The shock of these things must be engraved unforgettably on our memory. The dreadful nucleus of these events is something we have to recognize even when it tries to hide behind the glittering armor of the most idealistic words and goals.[1] Not the program but the deed discloses what powers drive the heart on and control it.

All we do is bound to be powerless and evil if the heart is parched and diseased, burdened and faint, or worst of all, if it is hostile, filled with the impure fires and poisonous smoke of blind hate. Only an inner life

---

[1] A veiled reference to the totalitarian States.

that is recollected and that lives in the strength of concentrated peace, only a harmonious heart that does not disintegrate in quarrels and strife, can give proof of strength to act. For only good works are constructive. Everything else is destructive. Men can see the outward effects, but God tests and knows the inner recesses of the heart. He wants to lead our hearts away from murderous demolition to the living work of building-up. He alone knows how to guide them, just as a man guides streams of running water to one place or another in his garden. God wants to let all hearts flow together into *one* great garden, into the Kingdom of His unity, love, and justice, where everyone does what is good because his heart moves him to it and because the Spirit leads him and urges him on.

In the Bible the heart is seen as crucial in man's renewal. As the Bible sees it, everything of significance is decided in the inner recesses of the heart. From the heart flow not only the streams of blood that fill our veins—no, also the pure winds and waters of the Spirit. That can be seen in the contrasting statements about the heart in prophetic and apostolic writings: not that which enters the heart from *without* but that which comes from *within* the heart, from man's inner being, is what defiles him. It is false to maintain that man's nature can be influenced by food taken in by the body or by hygiene or by gymnastics. This is in distinct opposition to the Word and life of Jesus. It results in this thoughtless and deceptive saying

"A man *is* what he *eats*" being set up in opposition to the truth of Jesus. The adherents of this opinion have themselves had to realize only too often that the defilement of man's inner being lies deeper than in eating and drinking. The true food, the food of the Spirit, remains the decisive thing, though to be sure the abuse of eating and drinking through luxurious living can also burden the heart.

In truth it is quite the other way round: a luxurious and voluptuous life has its origin in the heart. What a man *is*, he *does*. There are deeper signs of this than menus and rules of hygiene. As long as a man thinks first and foremost of his health and his own well-being, he remains an unredeemed man with a sick and self-seeking heart. Because he loves his life, he loses it. Only when he gives it up, does he find it.

What has vital significance is what comes out of the heart to the light. Every sort of idolatry will inevitably be exposed. The words uttered by the mouth (the outward speech) come from the over-flowing of the heart (the inner being). What a man *speaks about*, he *is*—that is, of course, provided he is speaking from his heart. Nevertheless, the sincerity or insincerity of a man's words cannot be hidden in the long run. A watchful spirit, clearly discerning the spirits, hears the tones of the heart and sees the lights of the soul. All empty talk is useless, however lofty the words.

What use is all outward service to God if man's inner being, his heart, stays at a distance! Only what a man does for the Lord with all his heart has any value. What point is there in letting our feet take paths and steps if our hearts do not go along too! All that is done and carried out in imagined strength remains a mere nothing if the living heart does not beat and pulse in it. As long as a man's heart stays quick and alive, even the weakest man, the man least capable of heavy work, can have the strongest influence. The heart is the inner core that does not rest even when the outer man is inactive. God does not look at the outward appearance but at the heart.

The strength and the weakness of a man lie in his innermost being. His inner attitude, although it can indeed be hidden or disguised on the outside, nevertheless makes all the difference to his character. Only that which passes through one heart to another has any value or strength, because it comes from the heart. Whoever has experienced how complete or almost complete strangers open their innermost hearts to one another will feel again and again the genuine heartbeat in each true word and will turn away from empty words in which the heart does not speak.

The living Church receives its unity and unanimity from the continual outpouring of the Spirit. It is there that the harmony of all hearts reaches its climax, for there all have become *one* heart and *one* soul. And this they will be over and over again, every time they believe in the Holy Spirit. Whoever wants to forgive with his mouth only or preach with his lips only can give us nothing but disappointment. "A preacher must have a heart that is on fire before he begins to preach." With these words Francis of Assisi revealed the secret of his fruitful life. "For anything that is to move hearts must come straight from the heart."[1]

The heart is rich in strength. What a wealth and diversity of lively emotions are embedded in the heart! Many people associate the heart only with feelings. And indeed, language does not go far wrong when it speaks so often of the emotional life as the heart's affair. A man's best and deepest feelings are seated in his innermost being, but just as much so are his wickedest and most harmful ones. All true joy comes from the heart and fills it with jubilant exultation or quiet happiness. All genuinely good deeds touch the heart. Every joyful hope has its life in the heart. The refreshing of the spirit, and not only that but also the refreshing of the body and soul, is a gift for the inner life, for the heart. For the heart is grateful for every consolation that offers bread and not stones.

The heart really does have to fight against fear and unrest and against pain and sadness! Our times have shown us all too clearly that the heart does not burn with love and joy only. All too often it plunges into the consuming fires of discontent and hate. We must be surprised to the point of being horrified at how for one reason after another passion causes the heart to flare up in rage and distress! What a catastrophe it would be for the heart if it were to exhaust all its

[1] Goethe's *Faust*.

wealth on its conflicting feelings! And how deluding these storms are even though they are often only big enough to fill a teacup! Strong impressions produce shaking emotions. Miserable lusts cramp the heart. Deep emotion alternates with very petty feelings. It can happen that unclarified, unconscious, and sub-conscious feelings lead to something good. But often they veil urges that are dangerously apathetic and can lead the heart to destruction.

It is not true that the heart can only feel. No, the heart as the inner part of man is more than feeling: it is intention and will. It is the seat of all deep thoughts, which have meaning only if they move our inner being. "Great thoughts come from the heart." Everything that is great seeks the living core. The heart is not only inner feeling: it is also inner thought. There is a speaking and talking going on in the heart that tries to bring inner clarity to all its thinking. Reason is not alien to the heart. To be sure, there are some unreasonable hearts who show by their errors nothing but folly. But what the sensible and understanding heart thinks out is wisdom. It understands how to know and how to recognize the best counsel. Just in the inconceivably heavy things that war and its historical consequences bring upon us all, just in the incalculable and unfathomable tasks that confront us, the heart needs the greatest and deepest thoughts. These God alone can give.

There are indeed thoughts that will always be alien to the heart. There are indeed hearts that hate thinking. But without a certain rich and deep fusion of thoughts there is no fruitful inner life. The whole wealth of life intended for the heart is available to it only when the heart is ready to open itself to the deepest thinking and reflection. It is in the nature of the heart to think and reflect. "Your heart is you yourself. Blessed are you if understanding always dwells in your heart." Only the consecrated thoughts of a dedicated life lead to this deep understanding. True understanding is given solely in the thoughts of God, which turn His will into the holy "Thou Shalt."

The effect that thoughts have on the heart's feelings provides a certain criterion of their value, though not always an infallible one. As Ruskin expressed it: "Literature, art, science—they are all fruitless and worse than fruitless if they do not enable us to be glad, and glad of heart at that." A heart that is truly alive passes a kind of higher judgment about those intellectual ideas that cannot fit into our life at the moment, and perhaps never will. "Like a sun, the heart goes through our thoughts and on its way extinguishes one constellation after another!" Jean Paul saw his inner life before him in this picture. All knowledge that is related only to the thinking brain is dead, including mere intellectual knowledge of Biblical things. Such knowledge brings life into deadly danger unless the heart takes a stand and unless it is so moved and alive that it is capable of making a choice between light and darkness, bright and dark rays, evil stars and good stars. Only thoughts that have glowing warmth and strength penetrate a pure heart and stream out from it again. Mirza-Schaffy's search for a completely integrated inwardness comes to expression when he proclaims:

> Head without heart breeds bad blood;
> Heart without head is still no good.
> For joy and blessing to last forever,
> Heart and head must go together.[1]

This cooperation of two instruments demands an inner energy that can embrace and hold together what so often threatens to disintegrate. No heart is without energy. Yes, the heart is *will*. Just as God's heart—being love—is the will that gathers and the will for His Kingdom, and just as the heart of Jesus wants to gather in His outstretched arms everything that is to be united in His Church, so the human heart that is healed in Him is the clarified will to gather and unite. If our inner being is not to let the precious wealth of truly great thoughts go rushing by, we must have a heart with a will that is active and glowing, able to accept words of truth and hold on to them firmly, just as Mary did. A will that is weakened by brooding and a nature that is ruled by feelings have never yet been capable of anything great. Faith received the Word of the Holy Spirit into the heart. This is the only way the Word can penetrate our life.

[1] Mirza-Schaffy: name used by Friedrich von Bodenstedt, 1819–1892.

The ultimate nature of the heart is in fact its inner desire, and its yet deeper will. This will is able to comprehend all that is said and to transform it into dynamic life-values. All intentions and wishes have their root in the heart. There is not only desire in the heart: deeper than that lie its intentions and resolutions. With its will, the heart holds on to the objects of its love and devotion. It is the inner disposition, the deeper direction of will, that makes the character of the heart what it is. Where a man's treasure is—the treasure that fills his inner life—there is his heart also.

"There is something in every man's character that will not let itself be broken, that forms the backbone of his character."[1] This backbone that is inwardly so firm and stable is the moral, loving, and uniting will. Without a decided will there is no character. "Character is moral order."[2] It is all the elements of the heart, ordered according to the laws of divine and human morality, according to the will to unity, and therefore in the active Spirit of pure and warm love. The backbone of this order is the will. As *will*, the heart is the school of character. True, it needs the stream of the world in order to grow strong. The will has to prove itself in work that is a product of active love by helping to build up a life that is consistent with the unity it aims at. It is steeled for this task in the hard struggle against all powers that are

[1] Georg Christoph Lichtenberg, 1742–1799.
[2] Ralph Waldo Emerson, 1803–1882.

opposed to unity. But if the will is not rooted in man's inmost being, in his heart, he will swim with the stream and cease to be a character.

If it is true that character depends on personality, then personality has its life and strength in the inner will. Only in the inmost recesses of the heart does one become truly free. It is only there that a decisive attitude is taken, one that means either moral firmness or a spineless unfreedom. It is the direction the inner attitude takes that makes the personality. As long as this direction seeks nothing but itself, it will lead the personality astray. Personality is "the greatest happiness of earth's children" only when the will no longer seeks itself but comes into action and sets to work for what is greatest of all—God's unity in His Kingdom and His Church.

In the last analysis, it is only in deeds that the personality reveals the inner attitude. Only those actions that require the concentration of all the heart's energies can be called deeds. *The* true deed is the uniting of all genuine powers of each individual, bringing togetherness and community to all men: the Kingdom of God among men is the concentration of all their powers in united deed. Only when we do not seek our own advantage but that of another are our deeds in keeping with the powers of God's Spirit at work in us: when in our deeds we sacrifice our own life so that community life may be established in unity, purity, truth, and righteousness.

The greatest deed of the strongest heart was accomplished by Jesus. When He died on the Cross, His resolute determination accomplished it. Here an energy of the will is revealed, a fire of love, a steadfastness in carrying out the perfect Will, such as can be found nowhere else. The struggle in Gethsemane and the cry of God-forsakenness on the Cross give a significant glimpse into what willpower was necessary for the heart of the Son of Man not to be broken by the anguish of His pain. Yet His love remained strong and unbroken till the end. In the very torment of death, the divine life in this Heart was marked by will to unity, consummation of the work of unification, trust in the Father, prayer for His enemies, concern for a criminal, tender care for His own, and the commending of His Spirit into the hands of the Father.

Just before that, His high-priestly prayer, as the profoundest speaking of the heart, had once more proclaimed unity to be the first and last will of Jesus. "That they all may be *one* as Thou, Father, art in me and I in Thee, so that in this, that they are *one*, the world may know and believe that Thou hast sent me!" The farewell words of Jesus—those words with such an inexhaustible wealth of thought, spoken to those who were His disciples in community and mission work—also revealed the Spirit in this relationship of unity. This Spirit, the Holy Spirit, was revealed to be the living representative of Jesus Christ, the Advocate of His Kingdom and His

Church, the personal power that thoroughly over-whelms in the conviction that the love that comes from unity is the truth. The Spirit of Truth is the One who calls to mind every word that Jesus said, including His last talks, which prophesy the ap-proaching Kingdom of divine unity. The quickening Spirit is the One who communicates the content and form of the future Kingdom for us today. Last but not least, the significant symbolism of the Last Supper proclaims the death of Jesus as atonement and liberation; it proclaims His death as the living creation of the new Body of Christ, which shall bring the whole of life into perfect unity.

All these words and acts show, in a profound wealth of feeling and will, the invincible power of God's thoughts in Jesus Christ, the power to accom-plish this deed, the most dynamic deed that ever a heart accomplished. As a revelation of God, this deed of Jesus demonstrates the concentration of all powers on the one goal that is their task. And this goal is nothing more and nothing less than peace, reconciliation, and uniting!

The heart is the inner character. In Jesus it is so firm and clear that in the sacrifice of His life He accomplishes the greatest deed of liberation, uniting, and gathering that can ever be imagined. In Jesus, the accomplished deed reveals His inner perfection. In every man, the nature of his deeds reveals his heart. Deeds reveal the character of the heart. If it is not clear and undivided or "single" as Jesus calls it, then the heart is weak, flabby, and indolent, incapable of accepting God's will, of making an important decision, or of taking strong action. That is the reason why Jesus attached the greatest significance to singleness of heart, simplicity, unity, solidarity, and decisiveness. Purity of heart is nothing else than absolute integrity, which can overcome desires that enervate and divide. Determined single-heartedness is what the heart needs in order to be receptive, truthful and upright, confident and brave, firm and strong.

Yet the Spirit of Jesus is seldom accepted and the strength of character that comes from Him seldom achieved. Weakness and dividedness of heart are to blame. How often the heart tries to overcome its own cowardice and faintheartedness through cold pride! The divisive callousness of pride is a weakness that destroys everything, making the inner self numb and stubborn, yet torn and disrupted too. The self-will that splits and divides itself has an arrogance that is the enemy of the love of God.

In vain the heart tries to close itself to the knowledge that it is too weak, too rotten and wicked, too disunited, too divided, and too hostile to help itself. For all its blindness to its own nature, and against its own will, the heart has time after time to uncover pride and arrogance, wickedness and cunning, ruthlessness and deceit, as the self-will and self-interest that continually divide it. Derangement of the heart can go so far in rigid obstinacy that all pretense comes to an end: God is tempted and cursed until darkness fills the heart's inmost recesses.

The heart, however, longs for the opposite—for a development of the inner life that leads to honest self-recognition, single-hearted simplicity, and unfeigned humility. In this spirit of modesty, the consciousness of one's own smallness unites with the divine call to true greatness. Such a development, which is brought about by God, requires a penetrating insight into everything that is base in one's own heart, an insight that in fact means a revolution in the heart. No one has an innocent heart when faced with this radical revolution.

Consciousness of guilt and unfulfilled longing for God, however, may not only soften the heart but positively tear it apart and crush it. Many people have shattering things to say about the consuming fire of this longing of the heart. Many a one calls it the deepest thing in himself, the thing he wants to gain a glimpse into:

> In my heart there burns an eternal lamp,
> quiet and steady;
> only once in a while it flares up high,
> rises to a flame,
> to a blazing fire
> that rages and consumes and destroys—
> then I summon all my energy,
> only one wish have I then,
> only one hope,
> only one thought — — —.

> And the eternal flame flickers and smokes
> for a long, long time
> until it is appeased and becomes quiet:
> my eternal longing![1]

The blazing flame of longing is certainly there, but it will have to flicker, restless and unappeased, and remain impure unless the heart submits to the inner influence of the sharp, clarifying Word and the cutting wind of the Spirit of God. Then the impure blaze can give way to the perfect light of the "Christ in us." Nevertheless, the heart is as weak as it is obstinate and only too used to its own divided and disrupted state, and it will not surrender lightly. It tries by every possible means to defend itself. It tries passionately to cling to self-chosen, human ideals, meant to bolster its self-will and hostile self-assertion—either alone or in community with kindred hearts who are equally selfish. But it is all in vain, even though the heart can cover up or postpone the decisive battle for a long time.

All mistaken attempts to lift the heart up in human, emotional "enthusiasm" for some god other than the "Father of Jesus Christ" have proved vain. In spite of every effort, all that the natural state of the human heart reveals is how far it has fallen away from God. Today more than ever this is unintentionally revealed by many movements. Those movements that arise from inflamed hearts pursue in vain the goal

[1] Michael Grabowsky, 1805–1863.

of unity and social justice by means of hate, injustice, and godlessness. Other movements pay homage (supposedly patriotic but in reality hostile and restricted homage) to a deity that is opposed to the living God—a deity that is alien to Christ and inimical to Him.

The cover must fall away—the cover that darkens the heart and restricts it to itself or to groups bound together by blood ties or a common lot. Nothing must hinder the outlook toward God. The God and Father of Jesus Christ can be seen only by looking with a resolute and unfaltering heart toward the perfect unity of His Kingdom, a unity free from all arbitrary boundaries, having as its one goal an all-embracing justice—the result of the divine joy of perfect love to friend and foe. This free outlook presupposes and demands a complete liberation of the heart from every false emotional tie, yes, a complete change of heart by means of the new birth that takes place through the Holy Spirit. The heart must not be allowed to remain as it is. It must experience the healing transformation that frees it from all rank and impure growth and all egotistical isolation of one or more persons—even of many people or groups of people—who set their own limits at will. The heart must be "circumcised," purified, and consecrated if it wants to be truly free. It must be freed from all the rank growth of self-will and self-glorification.

The Odes of Solomon, an early Christian song collection of the second century, witness in a profound way to this circumcision of the heart:

> My heart was circumcised and its flower
>     appeared.
> Grace sprang up in it
> And brought forth fruit for the Lord.
> For the Most High cut me by His Holy Spirit
> And opened my reins toward Him.
> He filled me in His love
> And His circumcision became my salvation.
>
> I hastened on the way of His peace,
> On the way of truth.
> From beginning to end
> I received His knowledge.
> I was firmly established on the rock of truth,
> Where He himself set me up.
>
> The Lord renewed me with His raiment
> And created me by His light.
>
> From above He refreshed me with immortality
> So I became like a land
> That blossoms and rejoices in its fruit.
> Like the sun upon the face of the earth,
> The Lord gave light to mine eyes,
> And my face received the dew;
> My breath delighted in the precious odors of
>     the Lord.
>
> He led me into His Paradise,
> Where the pleasure of the Lord abounds.
> I threw myself before the Lord

For the sake of His glory, and I said:
"Blessed are they that are planted in Thy land,
That have a place in Thy Paradise,
That grow like the growth of Thy trees
And have stepped from darkness into light!

"Behold, all Thy workers are fair
And do good works.
From unkindness they turn to the strength of
    Thy love.

"They cast off the bitterness of the trees
When they were planted in Thy land.
For there is much room in Thy Paradise,
And there is nothing that is useless therein,
But everything is filled with Thy fruits!"[1]

Therefore Fichte said: "As long as a man wants to be something for his own sake, his true nature and his true life cannot develop in him, and for this very reason he also remains cut off from blessedness." Fichte sees all selfishly isolated existence quite rightly as nonexistence because it is deadly restriction and a cutting off from the only true existence. It is only in blessed community with the divine Being that the greatest inner freedom can exist, replacing the unhappiness of sensual self-love and the insensitivity of moralistic legalism. Circumscribed self-love and heartless legalism are the enemies of the Gospel of

[1] See *The Early Christians After the Death of the Apostles* by the author of *Inner Land*, Eberhard Arnold (translated by the Plough Publishing House, Society of Brothers, Rifton, NY, 1970), pp. 246–248, Eleventh Ode.

unity and freedom. The true freedom of a heart
ruled by God does away with superficial legalism.
An inner urge that comes from perfect love replaces
it: the impulse of the Holy Spirit that leads to the
divine order of a common life in complete community.
Here all isolation and all arbitrary limitations are so
thoroughly overcome through the unity of the Holy
Spirit that the Church and the Kingdom are proved
to be the only true existence, the only true life. For
it is God's love that reveals itself in the unity of His
Church and His Kingdom.

This experience of God is that decisive enrichment
of the inner life without which even the most gifted
heart must starve inwardly. The inner acceptance of
the Living One means rebirth for a dead heart, so
that it then becomes a new, a different heart. It
cannot be a good and upright heart until it has
experienced a complete turnabout, a wholehearted
conversion that leads it away from false narrowness
within its own self to true breadth, to the experience
of God, who is greater than our hearts. The heart
needs to be redeemed from its stubborn self-life
because only in community with the perfect life can
it be restored to health. The perfect life is love. The
omnipotent breadth and depth of God's greatness is
revealed as love. In Christ and His Spirit, a complete
uniting (as the Church and the Kingdom) is brought
so near to us by love that together we are able to go
this way of love.

On the path of faith, the heart of man is led away

from the inner resistance it puts up against perfect love, and closer and closer to openhearted, voluntary obedience. The obedience that springs from faith opens up to the heart of God and to the heart of His Kingdom. It is only through experiencing the free gift of God's love that the human heart can be purified of its stubbornness and despair. Only unfeigned love from the purest spheres can oust those hostile elements that are the opposite of love: self-will, which is wrapped up in itself, and impure passion of all kinds, which destroys root and branch its own life-energy as well as that of its victims.

The gift that comes from the purifying and liberating love of the Most High is grace. In this one short word, the Bible encompasses the wealth of God's heart, which wants to give itself to us in love. It is in grace that God draws near to us. The hardship of our times and the abundance of tasks it brings show us how forlorn we are in the world, and how helpless, without God. In judgment, grace becomes the deepest need of our hearts. It is only through the free, communal gift of the Holy Spirit to His Church that the hardship of our times becomes an invigorating mineral bath, immersing us in the salty strength of the future Kingdom of God so that in complete community we can carry out here and now the tasks of justice. The greater the need and distress become, the nearer draws the Kingdom of God. The nature of grace is disclosed in the bitter fate of One who was crucified, in the way He sacrificed Himself completely to the greatest of all tasks. When the heart experiences the freeing power of His death, Scripture calls it being sprinkled with the blood of the Redeemer. The heart, taking firm hold of the unity with Christ through His death, puts the whole of life into militant action against those powers that put Jesus to death. Consequently, this baptism of blood means not only being ready to die for Him, but something even more immediate—being prepared time and again to risk life itself in the fight against those powers that oppose the Kingdom of God. For us there is no other basis for true peace of heart than this fight to the bitter end. Right to the point of death by martyrdom, the strength for this fight is gained from unity with Christ in His death, from the direct nearness of God's heart. Only the Cross brings perfect trust in God. Here, in the sharpest judgment of His wrath over all that is evil, God reveals loving grace to all as His innermost nature.

God himself lives through His Spirit in a heart that is united in this way with the Cross. His love is poured out in it. In the midst of murderous opponents of peace and justice, a heart filled like this remains joyful in love, in a love that includes all enemies. To this joy and this love the martyrs of both early Christianity and radical Reformation Christianity have testified a thousandfold. This fundamental strengthening of character, proven at that time in death, lets the heart unfold all its powers-to-be with the zeal of inner fire in order that, in life as in death, they may make an impact on the whole world. The reason Christ died for all was so that those who live may no longer live for themselves but for Him who died and rose again for their sakes. (2 Corinthians 5:15) That the whole of life up to the very brink of death is meant here, life with all its capabilities and activities, is shown by the other word of the same Apostle of Jesus Christ. According to this word, the same people who have just previously let themselves be used in the service of unrighteousness from now on give themselves to God in the service of righteousness. (Romans 6:13, 19) For this is the only way the work of the Holy Spirit can and will be continually built up anew as it once was in Jerusalem, no matter how often Jerusalem is destroyed and no matter how often His Church is driven apart by violence.

This wealth of power and effective action up to the very threshold of death cannot be won unless, as in the primitive Church, complete inner concentration and perfect accord prevail in the heart. We know from the history of war that the strongest political power is nothing but a helpless mass of people if a united will is lacking or has been lost. Such was the case in the World War. Such was the experience of cities and countries in times of siege. And so, too, the Protestant princes and cities were once "wonderfully favored by circumstances" for the Smalkaldic War: never, since the time of the emperors of Hohenstaufen and the Salian emporers, had the tribes of North and South Germany united in such a compact mass against the crown. At that time too, a war council torn by conflicting interests was to blame for the inevitable catastrophe of defeat.

Consequently, only when the heart ceases to let opposing interests split it apart can even the richest powers and gifts be a help and blessing to it. If the heart wants to win the victories of a faith that has courage unto death, it needs the wholehearted decisiveness of a unified will. We cannot serve two masters at once. We cannot pursue two ideals. We cannot seek two goals in two directions. The Kingdom of God, as the final Kingdom, does not tolerate in any heart any other kingdom besides itself. The way of Jesus is the only way that knows no byways, no wrong ways, and no devious ways. However many roads may lead to Rome or anywhere else—there is only *one* Kingdom, there is only *one* way: the complete uniting of all believers in all the activity that goes on in the heart and in life as a whole. Through the decisive outpouring of the Holy Spirit, all believers became so much *one* heart and *one* soul that they proved the uniting of all their powers, not only in the Word of the apostles and in prayer, but also in the breaking of bread and in community—in full community of goods too.

Only when there is an integrated will that is decided for God and united with all similar wills can the heart profess to seek God and His Kingdom. He will reveal Himself powerfully only through those who have turned an undivided heart toward Him.

An undivided heart does not tolerate a divided life. Only he is truly with God who surrenders to Him as his King with all his thoughts and feelings, all his powers, gifts, and goods in order to live truly for *God*, as an integrated character with an integrated life. The whole heart has to be converted before it is possible to follow Him. Where the whole heart is turned toward Him, it means that a life that is undivided (with all the powers of the spirit and all the wealth and capacities of soul and body) devotes every area of its existence to His rulership and to the Church. That includes professional and vocational activity with all the skills involved in it; it includes our worldly belongings and all our temporal possessions.

Unless we stand firmly with God, we cannot carry out our service to Him; it is possible to do His will in everything only when we love Him heart and soul. No one can do this of himself. If we are going to give all our strength and goods, we need strength from the Holy Spirit. This strength does not proceed from us but is given to us in the Word of the apostles and in the community of prayer and the breaking of bread. Whoever knows what it is to pray from a simple, undivided heart becomes grateful to *God* for His works and words and finds his happiness in worshiping the greatness of God and doing His will. Nothing will be impossible to one who prays this kind of prayer, the prayer that listens to *God* with heart and soul. Such prayer gives the inner life the boundless wealth of the truth of God. It leads the heart to the knowledge that truth is unshakable because it is the very essence of life. It has the power to accomplish everything. The impossible becomes possible. Unity is given a place in a torn world. Community in the fullest sense is created and built up, causing the unity of God's Spirit to shine out in man's work and production as the reality of the Church, as the City on the Hill.

If we want to wage the spiritual wars of Jehovah and to win the land for Him, we must acclaim Him with our whole heart! When His will rules in our heart, He will give our inner being a wealth of experience and action that it can attain only under God's rulership. It is only when our heart is filled with and ruled by Jesus Christ as our Master that we can be equipped and qualified for the great tasks that will inevitably confront us in the difficulties of these times and the hardships of the future. What these tasks comprise is nothing less than the call to the Kingdom of God and the task of His Church.

# SOUL AND SPIRIT

The question of life and death is bound to concern us more than ever before: war has brought death to so many who were in the prime of life, and crime against life has increased atrociously, as has crime against the life of unborn children. While the question of life and soul is one that men have wrestled with throughout the ages, the seriousness of the present time should make everything else drop into the background so that we can concentrate fully on what soul, spirit, and life mean to us.

Is it not one of the most astonishing facts that death should overcome life? No child can understand death. Least of all can he see how it is possible to kill men in the service of a higher cause. But even apart from this, to a child the thought that human life can one day come to an end is always unreal and contrary to the truth. The unnaturalness of dying is too remote from the simplicity of his affirmation of life. For the same reason, the heathen of old with their zest for life believed in the immortality of the soul. Likewise Goethe, who was very much akin to them, declared his life conviction to Eckermann: "I agree with Lorenzo de Medici that all those who have no hope for a life beyond are dead to this life as well." Life itself witnesses to its own invincible power. Hope is the hallmark of all living things.

As long as we want to deny that life is eternal, everything that belongs to life remains cloaked in tormenting riddles. Eternity remains the deepest longing of the human spirit. When man knows that he is an immortal being, everything he experiences is great and understandable; when he sees himself as mortal, it all becomes dark and futile. If there is no other future and no other world (which is bound to be victorious because it is the better world), then the injustice that prevails makes nonsense of human existence by giving final victory to "the worst of all possible worlds."

In the inner and outer circumstances of his life, every living person can learn to recognize this other world. Fichte has declared that we only need to rise to the consciousness of a pure, moral character to find out who we ourselves are and to find out that this globe with all its glories, that this sun and the thousands of thousands of suns that surround it, that this whole immense universe, at the mere thought of which our sentient soul quakes and trembles—that all this is nothing but a dim reflection in mortal eyes of our own *eternal* existence, which is hidden within us and which is to be unfolded throughout all Eternity. And the other way round, this is the truth given to mankind since primeval times: man's so very small world can be nothing else than a likeness—bungled, it is true, but nevertheless recognizable—of a bigger, truer, and more genuine world that is not limited by time and space. Our small world belongs to this bigger one and must correspond to it once again. For all of us, there is the moral code within us and the starry heavens above us to bring home a living intimation of this fact of Eternity.

Our life has its roots in Eternity. Its nature presumes imperishability. In space, the human spirit goes far beyond all comprehensible limits. And similarly, the absoluteness of the moral demands it makes knows no limit. The most certain of all certainties known by our spirit is this: that the ray of truth, the power of life, and the demand of the holy "Thou Shalt" come to us continually anew from a living world that lies beyond all space and nevertheless embraces all space. With this energy that comes from absolute authority, the human spirit follows the stream of time long before the beginning and far beyond the end, going outside all boundaries. This is the spirit's most crying need: the origin of all things before the beginning of time and the goal of the future at the end of time.

The thirsting soul pants for its original fountain-head and for the estuary toward which it streams. If it has awakened to consciousness of its true self and its divine destiny, it perceives in death an enemy of life, an enemy that is unnatural and that fights against the very nature of things. And it sees the same in everything else that tries to sully and destroy the clarity and purity of the Eternal. Everything in our present time and in our earthly space that opposes the soul's holy "Thou Must" and "Thou Shalt" must and shall be overcome (as the soul ultimately believes it will be) by the Kingdom of God at the end of all ages and beyond all earthly things. The "heavenly Kingdom" of the *other* world intervenes in temporal and earthly life as the power of the *future* world. It wants to transform life here and now according to the image of what is beyond and to come. This happens as soon as and as long as the soul lets faith rule in it, whenever and wherever that may be. This other life, which is already possible here and now, means freedom for the soul. But there will never be any such soaring of a free soul as long as an atmosphere antagonistic to life both robs it of its breath and obscures its view into the Eternal and Everlasting.

The freedom and power of a believing soul goes so far that it expects—with the prophetic Spirit— a holy transformation to justice and unity. It expects this also for every detail of material existence in space and time. It is in the hope of the Kingdom of God that the soul discovers its life. To the soul, the end of all the ways of God is unity in a tangible and visible form. For that reason, the Bible traces the death of the body back to the fact that sin as separation— as division and isolation—has brought a fatal breach into the living cohesion of creation. To the soul, evil is a power hostile to life, one that carries with it the danger of eternal death by separating man from God and man from man. Sin is crime against life and love. That was the reason why the first son born to those human beings who separated themselves from God inevitably became his brother's murderer.

Nevertheless, the ancient Scriptures of truth maintain that it is impossible to extinguish the life that God has given to man out of His own nature. From generation to generation, physical death comes to every man as a consequence of separation from God. The body does indeed die when the soul leaves it. The body that is left behind without the soul must fall to dust. Death can never deny that its nature is to separate by division and disintegration, and this it has proved since the very beginning through man's separation from God. Yet death is not annihilation.

The writings of both the Old Testament and the New Testament speak again and again about the souls of the dead. Every living soul has a capacity for future life. All vital movements of mankind look to the future. Whenever the soul comes to new life in the Spirit, it waits for God's future. And even if the soul cannot believe wholeheartedly in the coming Kingdom, faith tries to salvage this or that small fragment of the world-to-come and then clings to it all the more passionately. If people are not yet ready to fight and die for the final Kingdom of love and justice, they cling to a communistic State of the future or a Third Reich of national freedom and racial alliance. And in the same way, a remnant of faith in immortality and the other world emerges again and again, even in the most unbelieving, and this they can never lose entirely. Something in our being is meant to continue as an active force forever. Our divine Home calls us homeward. The spirit wants to return to God, in whom it has its origin. And though God himself is not yet recognized, there is at least an attempt to represent a little of His infinite significance even when it is done by idolatry.

Man today, too, has every reason to recall the faith in Eternity and Infinity that characterized the early Christians. If he wants truth and seeks it regardless of the unfounded prejudices of our time, he must and will recognize that here among the early Christians a glimpse into ultimate reality is given. In the face of this reality, no living soul can maintain its opposition. For here the soul is face to face with the life-giving Spirit of Jesus Christ. He who believes in Jesus will live even though he die. And the day is coming when he will awake and arise to a perfect life in an immortal body. The spirits of the just who have departed this life are at rest in the Living God and wait for the day of His future. The character of this perfect life in the Kingdom of God is shown by the parable of the Wedding and its joyful uniting, by the comparison with the Meal of Fellowship, and by the establishment of the thrones (Revelation 20:4); it is a life ruled by a love and a justice that bring about complete unity. In this Kingdom, at the end of all things, the one Holy Spirit will master and pervade everything. What constitutes life *now* is the soul (that is, the life) in the blood (Leviticus 17:11, 14), but *then* it will be the spirit, and instead of ruling over the soul's *human* body, the spirit will rule over a *spiritual* body.

In the Kingdom, the blowing Spirit takes the place of the coursing blood. The Spirit does away with fluctuating emotional ties and puts in their place a unity that He keeps constantly alive, a unity that is just as active as it is perfectly clear. In such a Body of unity, those who are at all times united in their Master and serve Him under His rulership live in a radically different way from those who, far away from God, are going to ruin, body and soul. Because these last have rejected the unity of life, they themselves have chosen death and separation. But even this second death cannot mean annihilation: even this death must show that its nature is separation and division. No more dreadful fate for a living soul can be imagined than to be cast out for all Eternity from the life that is in God.

To be excluded forever from the center of life is eternal death. Hell is nothing but the continuation of the lives of those who live for themselves. Their whole existence consists in the worm of decomposition and decay, the worm that does not die, the burning and consuming fire that is not quenched, and the judgment that means dissolution and separation. Simply because he had kept his riches to himself, the rich man—outside whose door the beggar Lazarus lay— met this eternal death. Ignoring the need of others, he had enjoyed his riches as his rightful possession. The only thing he had neglected to do was to give up all his goods to become one with the poor.

Only the man who sells everything and gives it to the poor can gain treasure in Heaven, which is none other than life in God. Jesus challenges every rich young man to this absolutely necessary action. Only in this way can he join the itinerant, property-free community of Jesus, the unity of those who follow Him. Humanly speaking, to go this way is and always will be quite impossible for young or old who own something valuable. But with God all things are possible. History proves it. Wealth is death because it isolates the heart from the need and distress of men and so isolates it from love. But God will and can give life even to the richest by calling him out of this death. He frees him from it by leading him to the love that surrenders everything in perfect trust.

How does it happen that God with His unlimited life takes hold of our limited existence and fills it? We must be perfectly clear about the answer to this question and all its consequences. God is life. Only in Him do we live, move, and have our being. Physical life throughout nature, like all life, has its origin and being in God alone. God does not disown His creation. He will lead it through fire to a new day. But the soul of man owes its decidedly unique life in a very special way to a direct communication from God. It is from God that we have the breath of life. He is the Father of Spirits. Just as He created the hosts of Heaven with His breath, so on earth man received spirit from Him in the same way.

The life of man is not limited to the blood that courses through his veins. The blowing breath of God, breathed into him as spirit, is deeper. It is this spirit that takes up a man's calling in life. It is the spirit's calling that has to determine the life of the human soul. The blood must not be allowed to rule over this calling. It has to serve it. Otherwise it ruins it. It is not without significance that in the first pages of the Bible the word *spirit* and the word for *soul* interchange in describing God's act of creation that breathed His breath into man.[1] The breath we have from God is spirit *and* soul. For this spirit that was breathed into our soul is the soul's unique life, its deepest life.

It is man's spirit that controls his soul and gives it distinction. Here is the boundary line between man and beast. Animals too have blood and a soul. What they lack is the spirit, which is more than reason and understanding. The shedding of the blood of animals is a responsible business, but anyone who sees the sacrifice of slaughtered animals as similar to the killing of men and can see only a relative difference between these two things—a difference of degree—has betrayed the spirit that God has given to man, and man alone, of all terrestrial beings. Man has been placed above the animals. The spirit of man

[1] This is more true in German than in English translations.

is meant to rule over the animals. However, he can do so only under one condition, and he can accept the ultimate sacrifice from them—the sacrifice of their blood—only under this one condition: that his life is given to the tasks of the Spirit and that, as God's image, he conquers the earth for God's Kingdom. But whoever kills man lays violent hands on the countenance of God. He commits a sacrilege against the task of the Spirit, for the Spirit wants to bring all men together and unite them. For no man is without spirit. When men cooperate with every breath of God's Spirit, it becomes impossible for them to fight with murderous intent and kill each other. Man is given to man to become united in life, because human spirit belongs to human spirit. The Spirit of God unites one human spirit to another by ruling over them.

The spirit of man is meant from now on to rule as the higher power over all lower powers of the soul and unite them under its dominion. This was known as early as Aristotle. It is simply impossible for a mere product of the soul's lower faculties to be the distinguishing feature of the human soul. The spirit cannot deny its origin. Therefore for a man to be ruled by his blood or to allow base or superficial things to satisfy him completely is seen as unworthy of man. Everything that betrays and destroys community in the Spirit is seen as base. Therefore we see as bestial and worse than bestial every debasement that takes place through the unbridled urges of the soul in the blood. More than any madness, it tramples the higher calling of man in the dust.

The human spirit has the very greatest of destinies: God and His Kingdom. Like the satanic spirit Lucifer, however, this spirit with such a high destiny has turned away from the Highest and precisely for this reason has become a rich breeding ground for the antigod principle. Separated from God, man seeks himself and his own kingdom. From now on he professes what is high and noble but without the rule and unity of God. He strives for the exaltation of man without giving recognition to God's deeds. He lives for human self-redemption, without honoring and accepting the deed of Jesus Christ and His redemption. For the people of his own race and blood and his own class, he is ready to sacrifice human life, rejecting God's Kingdom and God's people.[1]

In these days of ours, it should be plain to everyone that all these ideals of the human spirit that are separated from God have come to nothing. They have come to nothing in their concept of world peace without Christ. They have come to nothing in their efforts toward justice and freedom without His Kingdom and His Church. They have come to nothing in their illusion of an international unity without unity in the Spirit of Truth. Prosperity in a people united by race is founded on property and selfish advantage. In just the same way, the worldwide economic unity of high finance has been built up on the material

[1] A reference to Aryanism and political Communism.

prosperity of individuals and their mutual advantage. Even a proletarian Internationale composed of various elements has used its solidarity much more for material advantage in the present, for a fraction of the underprivileged (even if it is a large fraction), than for the justice of the future that shall embrace all men.

Now when in the face of all this, the policy of isolation makes nations try to close the frontiers of the earth in an effort to establish their economic self-sufficiency, they deny that the earth belongs to God. They deny that God's will is to be the God of all people and that the will of His Kingdom is to unite all nations in mutual service and make the products of their work the common property of all. It is impossible, though, for mankind to become an integrated world society, a world community of the Spirit, unless it allows God's Spirit to reprove it, judge it, and rule it. God's rule, however, means that no one seeks his own advantage anymore, that no one seeks privileges for himself anymore, and that self-preservation is nowhere placed above the Spirit's cause—that of unity.

Right up to the present day, there is no political element of worldwide importance that follows this way of *God's* world-rulership. Consequently, every great movement with a hope for justice has inevitably met defeat again and again. In just the same way, every kind of national self-redemption has come to grief—and will repeatedly come to grief—because, in setting up an idolatry that is supposed to bring recovery to the world, it rejects and even spurns the very nature of divine liberation and healing.[1] As long as the rulership of God and His Kingdom are put in the background, efforts toward human progress of any kind will inevitably break down over and over again. All human efforts toward salvation are doomed to fail because, in their delusion, they presume to lead men to the heights—not with God, but with the power of idols. Faith in the masses, faith in blood, or faith in any other power that is without the Spirit of God, will be annihilated in the fire of the future.[1] All kinds of false beliefs break down under the horrors of war, but annihilation in the fire of the future will be still more thorough.

However, what remains indestructible in all the waves of battle that surge around us is the spirit, which will be the first thing in man to surrender to God's will. Here and there in all parties, the inner depths of the spirit are already beginning to open up. The spirit is awakening. Its will is aroused. It is still blinded by a confusion of spirits. It is still benighted by separation from God. But the hour is near when the spirit of man far and wide will be gripped and called by the Spirit of God.

The fact that the soul is tied in two directions is the cause of all the confusion that hinders this call. Through the spirit the soul is drawn to God on the

[1] A reference to Aryanism and totalitarian States.

one side, and through the blood it is bound to what is physical and material on the other side. In this dilemma, it remains dangerously exposed to unspiritual movements that continually attack it and try to sever it from the Spirit of God.

The physical and material is not the real enemy of the soul. It is merely the area that the soul has to bring under control as its task. Rather, the enemy of life is the corruption of soul that thwarts all efforts to accomplish this task. It is only since the soul has become degenerate that it has come under the oppressive power of the physical and material. From the beginning, it has been an accepted fact that body and soul pervade each other, but originally it was the spirit that was meant to rule over body and soul. Through repressing the spirit, the diseased soul has brought things to such a pass that the spiritual life nowadays is enslaved to physical conditions.

Our turbulent times today show much more clearly than more settled times can how no human spirit and no movement coming from a human spirit can ever boast of being free and independent through its own efforts. Man today is bound to the peculiarities of his race and nation; he is dependent on his economic situation and on his privileged—or underprivileged—education for his mode of life and physical strength; he is influenced by powers of suggestion coming from other people or from big national movements; not least of all, he is at the mercy of his natural disposition and his own psychophysical makeup; and he is bowed down on all sides both within and without under the power of forces that are hostile to the Spirit. All this is in itself proof that only God and His Spirit can bring freedom.

Any other freedom is a lie. The only possible way for the individual consciousness to become free from its servitudes and for the nations and the masses to become free from enslavement is through the community of human spirits with God's Spirit! Without this direct oneness with the whole, the individual soul remains enslaved, impoverished, and limited, just as does the collective soul of a family group, or a nation, or a class, or any other combination. All other combinations of men and strength lead deeper and deeper into ruin through constant escalation of mutual hostility. The highest and the ultimate in true liberation and uniting will be given to man only when the highest unity in God takes possession of him.

The human soul is a subordinate unit of consciousness, which in spite of all ungodly association with kindred lives, remains lonely and thwarted until it is bound to the superordinate unity of God. Fechner catches in men's seeking a glimpse of this highest unity of consciousness.[1] He sees it as the truly Eternal and Unchangeable, as the One, always true to Himself, who wants to be at work in rich variety and infinite diversity. Without God's Spirit we are changeable, inconsistent, and unstable—unbalanced and

[1] Gustav Theodor Fechner, 1801–1887.

out of proportion and torn and hostile within ourselves and among ourselves. Therefore it must be an experience of absolute unity and, at the same time, absolute disparity that unites the consciousness of the soul with God.

With such an experience, Eternity is born in us, and we have to consecrate our life with complete dedication. For this experience becomes new every day—a continual new beginning. As often as we lay hold of life in God, these new beginnings, these deeds and actions, are stamped with the seal of Eternity. Eternity penetrates time. The Spirit of Creation seeks out the life of the earth. Being filled with what God's eternal will decrees can never result in alienation from life. On the contrary, the Spirit of life can lead only to an unfolding of powers in all the diversity of all life's relationships. In our families and in our professional lives, in our work and in our whole sphere of activity, in society and in community, the creative Spirit wants to shape life into a productive unity.

As Jacobi has expressed it:

> The spirit that aspires to God
> Must indeed lift himself from the dust.
> But if on *earth* he does not truly live,
> Neither will he live in *Heaven*.[1]

Whoever is gripped by God's Spirit turns to His creation with all the interest that comes from God's love. His life has one goal: that God's Kingdom shall come

[1] Friedrich Heinrich Jacobi, 1743–1819.

to rule over the men on earth, that His will shall be done in our world just as it is in the Kingdom of Heaven, that His name shall be honored in active recognition of His nature, that His holiness shall never be desecrated by any unholy action anywhere—rather, faith shall bring forth a love that makes God's nature recognizable through deeds.

It is through being ruled more and more by God's Spirit, and in no other way, that the spirit of man can get nearer to this high and final goal. Only the spirit that is ruled by God is able to see into the depths of revelation. Revealed truth was given to man on the basis of the prophetic Word in Jesus Christ and in His apostolic Church. God's Spirit wants to lead the human spirit into this truth in such a way that men's lives become filled and determined by it.

The Word of God pierces a man until it divides soul and spirit asunder in order to let him recognize without a shadow of doubt the unspiritual sensuality of the unredeemed life of the soul and in order to set his spirit, which thirsts for freedom, face to face with God's Spirit. If in our inmost being, the spirit (as the breath of God) does not stand out quite sharply and clearly in contrast to the soul (as the impure stream of our blood), we remain in the torpor of spiritual death. Those emotional people who allow the unpurified life of their soul to rule them are unable to receive the divine Spirit. There is no sharper contrast to the consistent wisdom that comes from God than the worldly wisdom of the soul, which inevitably gets entangled again and again in untruth-fulness when it tries to bring some semblance of harmony to its contradictory aims.

The way the world situation develops during war and the aftermath of war should make it clear to the blindest of the blind that the natural life of the soul is diametrically opposed to the life that comes from God. Men believe that they have all the life they need in human evolution, in patriotic efforts, or in the struggle of their class for justice, just as if they did not need God. Men presume to lay claim to things that are God's alone. They even want to decide over the life and death of people and nations. They forget that it is the Lord who kills and makes alive. They scorn the fact that God is life. Yet He alone is Lord over life and death. Whoever honors Him in Christ cannot kill any man or judge any soul. Men lose all feeling for the fact that life lies in His hand—that His decree alone has the right to determine the destiny of the soul. People lose all fear of Him who can destroy body and soul. Men stand before His judgment without awe. They lose all reverence for God.

We know that if the sun were extinguished it would mean instantaneous death for all life on our planet. We admit that an old riverbed will not have running water anymore once the stream has been diverted. It is clear to everyone that even the best water becomes a miserable slough if it has become disconnected from its source. Yet we have tried to deaden our conscience whenever it said that every lack of reverence wounds our soul with a mortal wound. We have wanted to forget that sin—violation of life—brings death to the soul: it is the destruction of man.

Unspiritual desires and the lies and deceit that go with them, hostility and the lust to kill, Mammon and possessions—they all fight against life and soul. For these are the forces that constitute the power inimical to life—that power that has separated itself from God. The spirit of man is bound up with the life of the soul: it cannot be pure if the soul does not live in God's purity, and every time the soul touches the rottenness of impurity and allows itself to be contaminated, it is not living in God's purity. The spirit is then tainted along with the soul and therefore is incapable of redeeming it. The spirit of man lives in his soul. Everything that goes on in his soul influences his spirit and all the movements of his spirit.

We should not imagine that the spiritual life can work independently of the world of body and soul as if it were in splendid isolation on an island, untouched by all that the soul experiences on the mainland. It is the entire atmosphere coming from the whole of a man that influences his thinking. No vibration of the soul leaves our spirit unaffected. During the second half of the nineteenth century, the brain was thought to rule from an autocratic throne over the life of the spirit. Recent research has dethroned it. The brain does not determine the soul's character or man's attitude as a whole with all his most important impressions, feelings, and emotions. A sick soul can have a brain that is completely intact. The soul can be healthy even when the brain is diseased.

The Bible of old is right in saying that the heart, the blood circulation with all the special organs belonging to it, and especially the different strains in the blood itself determine the character of the soul—the spiritual personality of a man. (Deuteronomy 30:14–20; Proverbs 15:13) Blood and heart can disperse melancholy of soul and depression of spirit and provide the necessary constitution and frame of mind for the highest literary achievements and even for abstract intellectual ones. Granted the brain is a very important organ for the intellectual work of comprehending, thinking, and remembering, yet it is simply *one* of the tools in the life of the soul and the spirit. It is only one of its workshops or transmitting stations, which in a special way reflects the life of the soul and the life of the spirit; it is their place of action.

We must not confuse the spirit of man with brainwork in general or with its more specialized intellectual functions. The human spirit represents much more the "practical reason" of the holy "Thou Shalt," which, according to Immanuel Kant, makes its incontestable demands with the firmness of "Thou canst because thou shalt."[1] The spirit of man is not to be

[1] Immanuel Kant, 1724–1804.

found in any specific place in his body. The bearer of man's entire soul is the whole body of man. The human spirit and the basic character of the spiritual attitude are breathed into the entire soul as its profoundest and most divine element. This spirit is able to prove itself extremely independent of the body, and superior to it, as soon as it has experienced a decisive liberation.

Such a liberation remains an impossibility, however, unless it embraces all areas of the soul. The human spirit is inevitably affected by any lack of freedom and any defilement of man's life. The soul embraces all manifestations of life. It is the bearer of everything that is alive in man. The soul is the total consciousness of the individual: the combination of all his sensual perceptions as well as the concentration of all his higher and spiritual relationships. There can be no other life for the soul than in this consciousness with all it encompasses. In this consciousness, all we experience with our feelings, thoughts, and will becomes reality and knowledge.

The consciousness of man is that undefined place where all his functions and organs are to become a unity. Unity of consciousness is the secret of organic life. Unity of spirit is the secret of man's calling. In man as a living whole, we can recognize the body by the finger of the body pointing outward, the soul by the finger of the soul pointing inward, but the spirit we recognize by the finger of God pointing to His Kingdom.

The life in the physical frame—that which makes it into a living body—is its soul. In countless instances therefore, the translators of the old Scriptures interpreted the word "soul" as "life." The soul, being life, encompasses our spiritual existence just as much as our physical existence from birth to death. Whenever it is a question of preserving or risking life, of danger to life or loss of life, the word "soul" is used where we would expect the word "life."[1] That the soul is the life of an organism is testified by this fact: "The soul (that is, the life) is in the blood." (Leviticus 17:11, 14; Deuteronomy 12:23)[2] Just as our physical frame without blood has no life, the body without the soul is dead.

It is not by chance that the thought of blood that is shed is more horrifying to us than the thought of the graves of the slain. We could see this in our reaction to the news of the reddening of the Masurian Lakes in World War I. In spite of an obvious scientific explanation, the reddening of the so-called Lake of Blood and War in Siberia (which is said to grow deeper with every great bloodshed) also makes a deep impression on people's minds. This is simply because blood and soul—the red of this special sap and the tremendous fact of life—cannot be separated.

[1] This is not so true in current English although some English translations do use "soul" more than the Revised Standard Version does.

[2] Compare Moffat's translation of the Bible with the King James Version.

It signifies more to us to see life ebb away in a stream of blood than to stand in front of a corpse.

The physical body that has lost its blood has given up its soul. Mephistopheles makes Faust sell his life with a drop of blood because blood is streaming and flowing life. The evil spirit wants to have the whole of man. He wants his life. He wants his soul. For this reason he has to get hold of his blood. "Blood is a sap of quite peculiar kind."[1] Therefore, according to an old version of *Faust*, just as Faust is about to use his blood-filled quill to sign the contract with the Devil, the blood congeals on his scratched hand to give a warning. It congeals in the form of the words "Flee, O man!" This cry to take flight is forced from the blood by the imminent danger of being gripped by evil. The divine life has an energy that demands more than the blood in its weakness does. The Spirit demands that the soul resist to the utmost: "to resist to the point of shedding your blood in the struggle against sin."

Resistance unto death is exceedingly rare because the blood is bound up through the soul not only with the higher, spiritual life but just as closely or even more closely with confused feelings and the basest impulses. There is something in the blood that weakens. Those emotional people in whom the blood is not ruled by the spirit are easily led in their sympathies, becoming weak and unobjective. Because of their lack of strength for vigorous action and their

[1] Goethe's *Faust*.

limp, unmanly compliancy, they are easily led astray. The more lost a man is on the false path he has once begun to tread, the more does each successive emotional weakness cause his soul to wither away.

An enfeebled soul is swept along whenever the individual or the nation is roused inwardly by an appeal to the blood or by an insistence on blood ties. That is why mass suggestion is so successful. Whether it excites sexual life into degenerate licentiousness, incites the masses to war or civil war, or shatters business habits of trustworthiness and entices people to luxury and extravagant living—whatever it does, the surprising result is explained by the weakness of the emotionally unstable masses. Each time that such weakness of life stirs the blood, it reveals the tyrannization of the emotional life over the nobler element of the spirit—in actual fact, therefore, it reveals the ignoble servitude of man's highest possession to his lower nature.

An effective renewal of life can come about only when soul and blood are gripped and penetrated by the highest life, coming from the Spirit. This new life must come from the Spirit because only in the Spirit can freedom and clarity begin. It has to penetrate into the blood-life of the soul if it is to be a reality in life. For blood builds up the human body. Without the soul or life in the blood there is no organic connection between the spiritual life and the physical existence of the body. (Romans 8:11)

For this reason, according to ancient mysticism,

everything that has gained power over my blood has gained power over *me*. Here is the link between the inner world and the outer world. If we want to master things we have to pluck up courage, and take heart: "Blood is the sap above all saps. It can nourish dauntless courage in the heart."[1] The soul reveals the fact that the blood is the natural element of all our urges and feelings, including—not least among them—the sensual ones. Because the blood communicates with every power center of the body, a state of excitement in the blood is often an indication of an unspiritual life guided by natural instincts and impulses. The blood stream is the nitric acid that tests whether the spirit or the body has the rulership. Whichever of the two comes through this test has won the battle.

However precious our blood is to us and however sacred our blood ties must be, we need a life that is not guided by our senses and our blood but determined by the Spirit. The life of the blood can be as thoroughly decadent as it can be noble. It bears within it the seeds of corruption. Everyone who builds on the blood is building on shifting sand. Blood is unstable and perishable. Only the Spirit remains alive. The storm of the Spirit is stronger than any other wind. The life of the Spirit alone stands firm when all other life is doomed to destruction.

In these critical times we need more than ever a testimony to the truth that God has given an eternal

[1] From an old version of *Faust* produced in 1690.

life—one that cannot ebb away with the blood because it is God's life and therefore independent of the blood and the senses. According to the true testimony of the Spirit, this life is in His Son. It comes to us through the Holy Spirit. It gives our spirit testimony of another Homeland, different from the land of our blood. It makes us so really and truly sons and daughters of God that we can represent no other interests save those of His heart and His Kingdom. The Spirit leads us to a people quite different from the people of our blood. God's eternal life unites us with the people of God whose bond is not one of blood but of the Holy Spirit.

Only those who are prepared to risk life and blood can find this Kingdom of the Spirit. But others can and will not tolerate it that the spirit of this people conquers the land. The path this people treads is strewn with the dead. By what he does to God's people, the god of this world has to reveal himself as the Murderer from the Beginning. The Spirit of Jesus Christ has never allowed His Church to kill even one single person. His people, however, have continually been murdered just as Jesus himself was brought to execution by the best state (from the military and judicial point of view) and by the most outstanding nation (from a religious and institutional point of view), yes, even by the majority vote of those of His own blood.

Today also, men and nations, the State, and the institutional Church will not tolerate witnesses to divine truth. It is not only the Eastern State that cries out, "Away with Him!" Voltaire's "*Écrasez l'infâme*" is the cry of the West. Whoever wants to represent the witness of Jesus in word and deed must be ready for death anywhere. The reason is clear: witnessing to the truth tears down all the disguises that are meant to conceal the workings of the prevailing powers.

Jesus has brought us a revelation that destroys all delusions. It exposes the true state of the world and its kingdoms, its principalities, its god and spirit, as well as the true state of every single human being. It is only under His influence that we become free of the false idea that life consists in politics and economics, in power and property, in violence and the struggle for existence, in eating and drinking, in clothing and housing, in pleasure and variety, in honor and reputation. The body is more than clothing. The soul is the life and therefore more than food. The Kingdom of God is more than all the kingdoms of this world. The spirit is more than the soul. What does it profit a man to gain the whole world if he forfeits his life?

Life during World War I and the aftermath of escalating need and distress freed many from a narrow-minded, bourgeois misconception: that the creature comforts of a pampered mode of life (quicker transport and communication and a good income) are necessities of life. Moreover, many consciences have been awakened from their torpid sleep and kept awake as if by a constant thunderstorm, realizing that in the face of the increasing distress everywhere they have no right to hold on to a privileged way of life. Men have to come out of their castles and open the doors of their villas in order to search out and bring in those who have become destitute in the storm, those who are without work or home. A true life of community with God encompasses the inmost fortification of our stronghold as well as the outer fortifications. When our soul has been awakened to the Kingdom of God, the Spirit who rules from that Kingdom will have to tackle our existence and shape it according to His will down to the outermost details. His will is toward brotherly love. This transformation will be so thorough and complete that very few people have any picture of it.

However, before we can think of a new form for our outward existence, body and soul must be taken possession of by God and changed to accord with His image. We have experienced in the history of our times how impossible it is to reconstruct an outer existence and build it up when inner strength has gone into a decline. It is not only in the Russia and in the Austria of pre-World War times that we can see how little even such great empires signify when their inner character begins to break up. What is a kingdom that is divided in itself? "What does it profit a man to gain the whole world and yet suffer harm to his soul?"

Nothing is more necessary than an inmost renewal

of life. In this renewal our destiny, independent of all alien influences, shall unfold like a seed growing into a strong, firm tree, allowing our soul and its whole sphere of activity to become that which is intended. It is not in ourselves that we find the strength, inner peace, and freedom for the growth of this true and genuine life. Still less do these prevail in the world around us. Only the truly Living One can give them to us. Only He brings life, its fulfillment, and with it the active inner peace of His works. Only when He has become the loving, caring Overseer of our soul can it find the strength it needs for a new, free, and active life. Only He leads to a life in which the soul, freed from turning around itself and circling around false planets, can live and work from the center of life.

This life is God and His rulership. The light of the life given in Christ shines more brightly on our weak, selfish existence than the sun into our night. And just as the sun gives life and nourishment to this planet, Jesus alone gives His brother man the strength and nourishment to begin a real life and build that up in place of our previous sham existence. Jesus is the Bread of Life for which we hunger. He has the Water of Life for which we thirst. His life, which far exceeds all other possible ways of living, merits our dismissing once and for all our own weak, selfish life and all ideals restricted and determined by our blood. We must turn away from all the will-o'-the-wisps that flit around churchyards. We must hold

His burning light firmly in the hands of our heart because He wants to bring life into every grave. Nothing should be in our hands but His radiant life because this is victorious over all the worlds of death.

There is a legend about a soldier who for a long time seemed to seek nothing but murderous battle and vainglory. He devoted himself wholeheartedly to war, and even when he joined a crusade, vainglory seemed to be all he looked for. It so happened that he was the first to scale the walls of Jerusalem. He had the privilege of being the first to light his candle at the altar of the Holy Sepulcher.

This flame transformed his life, though. He forsook the princedom that beckoned him. He took the candle. It became everything to him. He rode and traveled roundabout ways to bring this flame to his people without letting it go out. He was looked upon by many as a madman as he held the burning light in his hands wherever he went, never taking his eyes off it. In the depths of loneliness, fallen upon by thieves, in want and exposed to storms, in hunger and privation and mocked at by the crowds, he concentrated on one thing: he shielded the flame. From then on he could never have another thought but to protect every tiniest flame of holy life. His life became a light of love in vigorously working for others.[1]

Whoever wants to protect this flame of God's love in his soul and guard the light of life will have to show

[1] Selma Lagerlöf, "The Sacred Flame."

this same attitude. Once we have kindled our life from the flame of the Crucified One, His Spirit with all its powers expresses itself in an undreamt-of way that we could never learn elsewhere. It is the torch of the Spirit that shows the way then. If we want to reach the goal of our destiny we can only do it by letting His divine love unfold from within to without.

Wherever this fire is kept burning in men's hearts, it means life for the whole world. It becomes a light on a candlestick set up for everyone. It is only a uniting in complete community of faith that will bring light to the whole world as the City on the Hill. Its innermost life gathers all members round the carefully protected central flame as round a campfire. Only he who protects this grail of the Church knows what wealth of life God sends out into all lands from His City.

Once we have come to recognize God as the only element of all true life, all inner powers of the soul seek to unfold in order to come fully and completely into action, concentrated on Him. The soul that is filled with God embraces the whole of life with all its activities, inner and outer, intellectual and physical. In order to bring life completely under the authority of God's vital power, its inner aspect must be brought under His influence first of all. The power of infinite life sinks its roots into the inmost depths of the soul before it has a strong and active influence on external life. The confession "Thou givest my soul great strength" can be made truthfully only when this strength has begun to reign in man's inner being.

The inmost heart of the believing Church, in which God dwells, is like a well-watered garden, full of quiet, peace, and security. Enemies cannot find the way in. A living wall of tall trees rooted in fertile ground protects it from the storms raging outside. The noise of the world outside does not penetrate into the secluded center of this garden, in which God's heart has its dwelling. And yet the gates of the garden stay wide open so that all that is living can go in. They stay open because all the powers and capabilities of the soul are sent out to share in all men's distress and bring them help wherever possible.

When we speak of the life of the soul, we usually think only of the innermost part of a believing spirit. But we have to remember that the soul embraces the whole of life. Then we shall understand why profound thinkers of all times have spoken about the inmost recesses and depths of the *soul*, about the bottom of the *soul* and the center of the *soul* rather than about any other seat of life.[1] The apostles of Jesus Christ exhort the believers to become new men in mind and spirit. What the believers have to do is to search their innermost being because their life in Christ shall be hidden in God, so that from the bottom of their hearts they can say, "I live, yet now it is no

[1] Where German idiomatic usage has *Seele*, English usage more often has the heart as the center of life.

longer I but Christ who lives in me." The spirit of a man is his inmost treasure. When it is illuminated by God's Holy Spirit, a man's spirit, and only his spirit, knows what is in him. When it is led by the Spirit of Jesus Christ, the spirit and only the spirit can become the lamp of God that searches all the innermost parts of the body.

By and large, the heart embraces the inner aspect of man. Therefore we find the manifestations of life in the heart—the thinking, feeling, and willing, the disposition and the character of the heart—ascribed to the soul as well. For the soul, as the life of man, by its very nature includes the heart as the inner core of life. We can imagine man's life as concentric circles of different colors superimposed on each other and enclosing each other. Our external, material body, part of nature as a whole, forms a comprehensive gray circle. A blue circle denoting the organic life we have in common with plants is just as big. The third circle, a red one, has the same dimensions and stands for the life of the soul in the blood, which, as a human person, embraces the whole consciousness. This last circle of life is characteristic of the animal kingdom as well.

With the smaller circles it is different. In contrast to the large perimeter three times covered, the heart forms a smaller concentric circle, perhaps best indicated by fiery coloring. This confines itself to the life of inner feelings and thoughts and activity of the will, that is, the deeper part of man's character.

This alone is enough to distinguish man from all other living creatures. The spirit of man, however, forms the center that dominates the whole. It is a secluded, inner circle, which in view of man's destiny should be colored white. This spirit is given solely to man. Schiller refers to this when he says: "Once I have searched the core of man, I know what he wants and what he is doing." It is this core that is all-important. God's Spirit wants to make His dwelling among men, beginning in the spirit of man.

The higher will of the soul is spirit. The *spirit* is the active and creative genius of man. The spirit is reason working constructively to meet the demands made by religion, ethics, and society. It is the spirit that directly perceives and experiences what is divine in the human heart. The soul on the other hand gets its feeling for life more through what is physical and determined by the blood. It includes all man's desires and longings and also that in him which is purely receptive. The whole reception of all the outer stimulations of life takes place in the soul. It remains more sensual, more closely related to the body, more strongly rooted in the body, and more firmly bound to it than the spirit. The spirit lives in the activity of the highest and freest relationships and aims of the will. It dwells in the most royal of all the chambers of the consciousness. For the spirit, the highest destiny is to be infused with divine Spirit, to be united with the Holy Spirit.

The consciousness of the soul is a living mirror of all the relationships into which the life of man is woven. The influence of these relationships varies greatly according to their intensity. It is in the life of the soul that the decision is made as to which feelings, desires, ideals, and thoughts we allow to cross the threshold of our innermost being.

As long as the feelings of the soul in the blood (which work in darkness) are controlled by the power of the Spirit ruling in our hearts, they cannot grow into base intentions or evil deeds. Yet we see in all the excitement of our times how these feelings wait for a moment when the image of God and His influence grow weaker in us. From that moment on, the lusts and false ideals of the blood (allied to other powers of darkness) can cross the threshold of our heart. They become the will to do evil, and then they unite in evil action. Sin has come. "Lust when it has conceived gives birth to sin; and sin when it is full-grown brings forth death."

Joyless lust for murder and hate, poisonous readiness to accuse one's opponents and use lies to disparage them, loveless joy in property and all personal privileges, impure and unspiritual lusts of the body—all these lie in wait for the *will* with insatiable greed. They have to capture the will with the dazzling temptations offered by stolen and pseudo-spiritual virtues before they can work their evil.

The soul is able to ward off these temptations only when the will that is good has found a strength to resist, coming from a firm foothold. It finds this foothold when the content of the soul, what fills the soul, is clearly and definitely of the Spirit. The will can reject all the enticements of seductive mental images; it can overcome all the temptations of murky ideals and aims; but it can do this only when—through being constantly reminded by the Holy Spirit—the soul's consciousness is firmly and clearly ruled by the unity that comes from the heart of God, by the unity of all the thoughts of His love, by the unity of all the pictures of His future Kingdom and its powers, and by the image of Jesus with all His words and deeds. "Strength of character depends on this, that a definite unity of images and ideas continually occupies the conscious mind, weakening any opposing images and not allowing them to enter."[1] If the seductive powers of other aspirations are not to gain admittance and rule over our will, then the innermost chamber of our soul must always be filled with the Spirit of Jesus Christ. The chamber where our spirit is enthroned must always be filled with all His thoughts and with His will, that is, with every impulse of His heart.

In such agitated times as ours today, the Enemy of our soul has a powerful band of accomplices that want to shatter and destroy it. But in the hush of night God speaks clearly and unmistakably to our soul to draw it away from destruction and make it His follower. He awakens the spirit and shows us the

[1] Johann Friedrich Herbart, 1776–1841.

way to life. He wants to fill the awakened soul with His peace so that dark powers have no room. When the soul cries out for God, driven to do so by the distress of our time, it will be led to the goal—to the Church and to the Kingdom—if by the will it is lifted up to Jesus Christ and remains concentrated on Him alone.

# BIBLE REFERENCES

The names and addresses of the communities of the Hutterian Society of Brothers are:

Woodcrest, Rifton, New York 12471
New Meadow Run, Farmington, Pennsylvania 15437
Evergreen, Norfolk, Connecticut 06058
Darvell, Robertsbridge, Sussex TN32 5 DR England

**Pleasant View, Ulster Park, New York 12487**